get a grip on
DREAMS
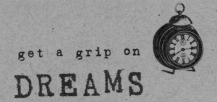

:Get a Grip on

DREAMS

MAEVE ENNIS + JENNIFER PARKER

METRO BOOKS
NEW YORK

This 2002 edition published by Metro Books,
by arrangement with the Ivy Press.

This book was conceived, designed,
and produced by
Ivy Press
The Old Candlemakers,
West Street, Lewes,
East Sussex BN7 2NZ, UK

Creative Director	Peter Bridgewater
Publisher	Sophie Collins
Designer	Angela Neal
Commissioning Editor	Peter Nickol
Picture Research	Vanessa Fletcher
Illustrations	Andrew Kulman

Metro Books
122 Fifth Avenue
New York, NY 10011

ISBN-13:   978-0-7607-3743-9
ISBN-10:   0-7607-3743-6

Reproduction and printing in China by
Hong Kong Graphics and Printing Ltd.

    5   7   9   10   8   6   4

CONTENTS

CHAPTER 1
To Sleep,
Perchance to Dream
6

CHAPTER 2
Interest in Dreams
28

CHAPTER 3
Lucid Dreaming
48

CHAPTER 4
The Creative Dream
56

CHAPTER 5
The Road to
Dream Interpretation
66

CHAPTER 6
Dream Themes
94

INDEX 190

CHAPTER 1

TO SLEEP, PERCHANCE TO DREAM

tick tock

we have our own internal clock

* It is not possible to write about dreams without also writing about sleep. We cannot disconnect the two. The people of classical antiquity believed that we slept in order to dream and thus to receive revelations from gods or demons. These revelations had an important purpose, usually to foretell the future. We still want to know what our dreams mean, and like the ancients, we want to feel that they are not just random musings of a brain "off-line," but that they tell us something about ourselves and our lives.

DO WE NEED TO SLEEP?

* We spend about 30% of our lives asleep, and about 25% of that time is spent dreaming. *This means that the average person spends 20–25 years sleeping and 5–7*

sleep helps to repair the body

KEY WORDS

CIRCADIAN RHYTHM: An internal clock that peaks during the day and slows down at night. Many of our body functions — temperature, blood pressure, metabolism, digestion, hormone secretion, and sleep— ebb and flow on this tide. Cues from the environment around us, especially the daily cycle of light and dark, are needed to keep this clock synchronized. Anything that disturbs this synchronization disturbs our sleep.

years dreaming. This may seem to some people like a waste of time, but it appears that we need sleep and we need it at regular intervals. It is not as beneficial for the body to have 4 hours one night and 15 hours the next, though few of us believe this when young. The body works on a 24-hour clock known as the CIRCADIAN RHYTHM, which is based on the revolutions of the earth as it orbits the sun, and the consequent periods of light and dark. *There is truth in the general belief that, for shift workers, the night shift produces less satisfactory work than the day shift. Work that requires a lot of manual input is about 20% less productive at night than in the day.*

sub-standard work?

night shifts are less productive

DO WE NEED TO DREAM?

✱ It would appear that we need to dream as much as we need to sleep. It is possible to stop people from dreaming by waking them up every time they start. *But it becomes increasingly difficult to do this unless we deprive them of all sleep.* People who are selectively deprived of sleep will increasingly go into REM sleep ("rapid eye movement," associated with dreaming) when allowed to sleep. This is called "REM rebound." *Generally we try to make up any REM time we lose.*

The function of sleep

Many theories have been put forward about the function of sleep. We secrete our growth hormones, which are responsible for tissue repair and renewal as well as growth, during non-dreaming sleep, so the most plausible theory is that sleep performs functions of repair and regeneration.

SLEEP OF DEATH

The ancient Greeks believed that the soul wandered during sleep. If the sleeper was awakened before the soul returned, he died or went insane.

very tired goalie

being physically tired does not necessarily lead to sleep

SLEEP AND DREAMING ARE NOT SIMPLE

* Sleep does not come about simply because the activities of the day require it. Whatever the condition of the body, we can choose, up to a point, either to sleep or not—although after a long time we may need some help to stay awake.

KEY WORDS

AUTONOMIC NERVOUS SYSTEM: The part of the nervous system that runs to and from the internal organs, regulating such processes as respiration, heart rate, and digestion. It also plays a part in emotion, speeding up the heart and causing perspiration during emotional excitement. In general it maintains the functions that keep us alive and protects our bodily resources.

WE ARE NOT UNCONSCIOUS

* Sleep is not unconsciousness, because we remember our dreams. *And sleep is not without physical activity; people thrash around and even walk and talk during sleep.* Nor is it necessarily without control, as some people can plan when they want to wake up. But this varies very much from person to person.

* When we fall asleep the body and the brain are not completely dead to the world. We are not unconscious. The body is kept going

our brains remain active even when we are asleep

by the activity of the <u>AUTONOMIC NERVOUS SYSTEM</u>, which controls the support systems of the heart, lungs, digestion, cell repair and replacement, and all the other systems needed to keep us alive and well. *The brain also continues to be active to some degree; when your alarm clock rings, your brain registers sound and responds by dragging you, no doubt sometimes unwillingly, from sleep.* Likewise, a mother will almost always hear her infant cry, no matter how soundly asleep she might be. *We are aware even when asleep of what is going on around us. Often we incorporate the sound of that alarm clock into our dreams, where it might become a fire truck or the end of a bout in a boxing ring.*

ring
ring

the noise of the alarm clock often becomes part of your dream

HEALTH WARNINGS

We may experience anxiety about a health matter in a dream, or may even dream that we are seriously ill, or about to be so. It may be that the dreaming brain is trying to tell us to act on information that our waking mind won't accept. For example, heavy smokers dream that they have chest or lung problems. Perhaps unhealthy foods should carry a health warning that says, "Listen to your dreams!"

HOW LONG CAN A PERSON STAY AWAKE?

In 1973, as part of a science project, 17-year-old Randy Gardener undertook to break the world record for staying awake. He stayed awake for 268 hours, more than 11½ days. And after sleeping just 15 hours he was back to normal again.

9

sweet dreams

WHAT HAPPENS WHEN WE FALL ASLEEP?

* It used to be believed that sleep was a unified state, that the brain switched from being awake to being asleep, and that no further change in brain activity took place.

EEG traces gave insights into sleep patterns

SLEEP STUDIES

With a series of ingenious experiments in the 1950s, Dement, Aserinsky, and Kleitman changed the way we look at sleep. Using an EEG machine and fastening electrodes to the scalp to record brain waves, near the eyes to record eye movement and on the chin to record muscle tone and tension, they showed us that REM sleep was a unique stage of sleep in physiological terms and that 80–90% of people wakened during this stage reported dreaming, while only 10% wakened during other stages did so.

BRAIN SCANNING

* In the 1950s three American scientists, **William Dement**, **Eugene Aserinsky**, and **Nathaniel Kleitman**, found that brain activity as measured by an ELECTRO-ENCEPHALOGRAM, or EEG, showed this not to be the case. *They found that sleep has five distinct stages, stages 1–4 and the REM stage, or rapid eye movement sleep, and that these occur in 90-minute cycles 4 or 5 times a night.*

* Observations show that on a typical night when a person is awake but resting, a steady wave pattern is detected by the EEG. These waves are called ALPHA RHYTHM. This is soon replaced by evidence of stage 1 sleep. About 15 minutes later

the sleeper enters stage 2, and again about 15 minutes later the emergence of some longish <u>DELTA WAVES</u> suggests entry into stage 3. Gradually over the next 15 minutes these waves predominate, reaching stage 4, the deepest level of sleep. The sleeper then goes back through the different stages from the beginning.

TYPICAL EEG RECORDS OF THE VARIOUS STAGES OF SLEEP

drowsy-8 to 12Hz-alpha waves

Stage 1: 3 to 7 theta waves

Stage 2: 12 to 14Hz-sleep spindles and K complexes

Stage 3: ½ to 2Hz-delta waves > 75mV

> ### KEY WORDS
> **ELECTROENCEPHALO-GRAM (EEG):**
> A record made by attaching electrodes to the scalp to measure brain waves
> **RAPID EYE MOVEMENT (REM):**
> During this period of sleep the eyes can be seen moving beneath the lids, as though the sleeper were watching the actions of their dream.

but I wasn't asleep...

✱ *About 90 minutes after the onset of sleep there is an abrupt change in the EEG. The sleeper will appear close to waking, the eyes move rapidly under the eyelids, there is loss of muscle tone, and the heartbeat is irregular.* This is REM sleep, also called <u>PARADOXICAL SLEEP</u>, because the EEG pattern looks very like that of a person who is awake and mentally active.

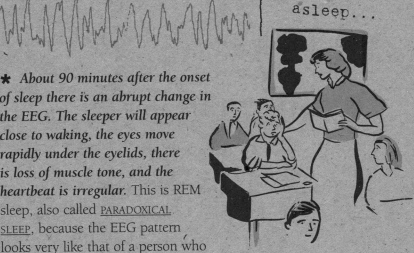

if you are awakened in the early stages of sleep, you do not realize you have been asleep

11

☆ what is this REM sleep?

WHAT IS REM SLEEP?

* This is sometimes called dream sleep, but this is a misnomer because we also dream during other stages of sleep. But it is the time when we dream most vividly, and we remember our dreams most clearly from REM sleep. It is also the sleep stage in which we dream the most bizarre dreams. People wakened from other stages of sleep will sometimes report dreams, but they are usually quite ordinary, more like daydreams.

REM sleep is the most interesting stage

REM sleep is very still and peaceful

The cycle

The cycle through stages 1–4 and then REM is repeated about 5 times during an average night. Most stage 4 sleep is accomplished early in the night, and most REM toward morning. But each cycle usually has all the stages.

AS STILL AS A STONE

* One of the big differences between REM sleep and the other stages in the sleep cycle is the change in body movement. We do not toss and turn when we are dreaming our REM dreams. We are in fact virtually paralyzed, having no muscle tone. *However, this is not a bad thing: Imagine how dangerous it would be if we could act out our dreams. Although the brain may send messages to the muscles to move during REM, these messages are suppressed at the level of the spinal cord.*

FALLING ASLEEP

* We do not gradually slip from wakefulness to sleep. *The onset of sleep is in fact quite sudden. It is seen as gradual only in retrospect.* Of course we gradually become sleepier and less restless as sleep approaches, but the border between wakefulness and sleep is quite distinct.

* Dement reports a study in which a volunteer's eyes were taped open (he assures us this is not uncomfortable). The volunteer was then asked to press a

heart attacks are more common during REM sleep

REM differences

Other differences are also apparent. Acid secretions in the stomach are increased, and heart attacks are more common during REM sleep. Also, it is only during REM sleep that men have erections. This is why men tend to have early-morning erections; they have awakened from REM sleep. It has nothing to do with dreaming erotic dreams, but is an involuntary response.

how can you fall asleep on your dinner?

the onset of sleep can be quite sudden...

switch every time he saw a bright light flash from a strobe about 6 inches away from his face. He pressed repeatedly and then suddenly stopped and was asleep. *The cessation of button pressing corresponded with a change in his EEG, which registered stage 1 sleep.*

have you been in REM sleep, Henry?

DREAMING ANIMALS

Bruno, wake up

* Almost all animals have REM sleep. If you watch your dog or cat sleeping you will notice that some of the time their muscles twitch, and if you look closely you will see their eyes move from side to side under the lids. It would appear that they are dreaming.

animals have dreams just like humans

REM sleep began when mammals began to produce live young

WHAT'S THE POINT?

* Why should animals dream? When dreaming a creature cannot hunt for food. It is vulnerable to its enemies, it cannot defend its young or its territory, and it cannot procreate. *Yet for about 130 million years, despite many evolutionary changes, REM sleep has persisted in most species.*

* Non-REM sleep developed about 185 million years ago, when warm-blooded mammals evolved from cold-blooded reptiles. Up to that point, early mammals (the MONOTREMES) reproduced by laying eggs, just as their reptilian ancestors had done. *Then, when mammals began to produce live young rather than eggs, about 50 million years later, REM sleep appeared on the evolutionary scene.*

METABOLISM

* Warm-blooded and cold-blooded animals have different metabolic demands. *During the day, cold-blooded reptiles have a ready source of energy in the sun, but at night, this is not available and they are vulnerable to attack.* Warm-blooded mammals, on the other hand, have a HOMEOSTATIC system, which maintains a fairly constant body temperature. But to achieve this they have to seek energy from food to maintain their metabolic balance. One efficient way of conserving energy is to have long periods of sleep.

* *But what has this got to do with dreams? Well, live-born young are very vulnerable. They have to grow and learn at a tremendous rate before they can survive on their own. There is a need for great development of the brain, especially in the early weeks. REM sleep is thought to play an important role in the developing brain in human infants, and the same may apply to animals.*

Brain waves

Brain-wave recordings taken from animals as they carried out activities essential for survival— such as exploring the environment, stalking, and killing prey—were found to exhibit a distinct pattern, called theta rhythm. This rhythm comes from a part of the brain called the **hippocampus** *(the Greek word for sea horse, which it resembles), known to be involved in forming long-term memories. Theta rhythm is also present during dreaming. So do animals dream of hunting and chasing, and why don't they run around in their sleep? When animals and humans dream in REM sleep they lose all muscle tone. They are in effect paralyzed. But a French scientist called Michael Jouvet found a means to turn this paralysis off in a cat. The cat, while still dreaming, got up and seemingly chased a dream bird and caught and started to eat it. The cat was acting out its dream.*

animals may
develop
skills
during
dreaming

MEMORY

* At the same time as Jouvet was examining theta rhythm in dreams, the American Jonathon Winson had found that theta rhythm was involved in memory and that the storage of memory was in the hippocampus.

it's all to do with the **hippocampus**

THETA RHYTHM

* Winson concluded that theta rhythm reflected a process where information that was gathered during the day, which was ESSENTIAL FOR SURVIVAL, was reprocessed into memory during REM sleep. Dreams could be how animals update their survival strategies in light of current experience. This is done when the animal is asleep, a time when the brain is free from outside distractions. _When animals dream they are rehearsing their survival behaviors._

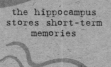

the hippocampus stores short-term memories

MEMORY LOSS

* The hippocampus is directly involved in short-term memory. Research has shown that it takes around 3 years for short-term memories to be properly lodged into long-term storage. No one knows for sure how memories are moved from one storage to the

no short-term memory

damage to the hippocampus results in a loss of short-term memory

other, but many believe that dreaming is involved.

* Winson has suggested that there is a system called NEURONAL GATING, by which chemically active neurotransmitters are either allowed to enter or denied access to specific areas of the brain. **The hippocampus is one of these areas.** When an animal is awake these gates remain closed, but when the animal falls asleep the gates begin to open, allowing the neurotransmitters to enter the hippocampus.

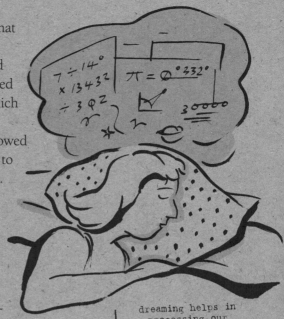

dreaming helps in processing our memories

By the time REM sleep appears, the gates are wide open and the waves of theta rhythm appear.

dreaming opens a kind of gate in the brain

* *Winson believes that this is true of humans also, and that dreams reflect a memory-processing mechanism inherited from lower animals, in which information for survival is reprocessed during dreams. He believes that this information could be the core of the unconscious mind. This link between dreaming and memory can be seen when we deprive people of REM sleep. They have difficulty in remembering what they have learned from one day to the next.*

KEY WORDS

HIPPOCAMPUS:
The most important part of the brain for processing and storing memories. The hippocampus is situated in the temporal lobes on both sides of the brain and is part of the system that is involved in emotion as well as memory.

17

SORTING AND SELECTING FOR THE LONG TERM

* According to Winson's theory, in order for a short-term memory to be firmly established in the long-term memory store, it has to be "dreamed" for about three years and then stamped into an area of the brain called the neocortex. However, if all our short-term memories were to end up in the neocortex it would need to be much larger than it actually is— so large, Winson suggests, that we would need a wheelbarrow to move it around.

SORT IT OUT

it's my overdeveloped neocortex

* So some sorting out must be going on. At some point or structure within the brain a decision must be being reached about what is important and needs to be kept and what is unimportant and can be thrown out.

* *Francis Crick and Graeme Mitchison (see page 46) believed that dreams were implicated in this process. However, their emphasis was not on selecting and recording but on unlearning and dumping. Many dream researchers now believe that dreams are involved in the storing of memories that are important to the individual.*

if all our short-term memories were retained our brains would be huge

PHYLETIC MEMORY

✳ But what decides whether or not a memory is important enough to go into long-term memory? Winson proposes something called PHYLETIC MEMORY, similar to Jung's idea of the collective unconscious (see page 43), which is the COLLECTIVE MEMORY of a species. Winson claims that dreams are a processing device that looks at new memories and evaluates them against a store of information that is already coded in the long-term memory, some of it from the early life of the species.

✳ In defense of his idea, Winson cites the case of the echidna, the spiny anteater. This small creature has an enormous brain relative to its size, but it does not have REM sleep. *Since it does not dream it needs a much bigger brain to hold all the information it needs over a lifetime.*

✳ This would suggest that, after millions of years, when human evolution stopped because it was limited by the size of the head, nature moved on and evolved another system, namely REM sleep. *But of course animals' dreams are different from ours, less complex and more linked to the collective memory. Our use of language and symbols means that human consciousness has evolved further.*

KEY WORDS

NEOCORTEX:
The thin convoluted surface area of gray matter in the brains of higher animals; also called the cerebral cortex

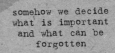

somehow we decide what is important and what can be forgotten

CLEVER HUMANS

We are able to assess the present, both awake and in dreams, in the knowledge of past experience and without having to refer to that "phyletic memory."

CONFLICTING IDEAS ABOUT REM

* In recent years there has been some criticism of the theories linking REM sleep, dreaming, and memory consolidation. Although Winson believed that Freud was right in declaring dreams the "royal road to the unconscious" and therefore meaningful, he thought Freud was wrong to see the unconscious as full of unfulfilled wishes, and dreams as disguised versions of these.

BRAIN SCANS AND DREAMING

dreams have no meaning at all

* Some modern scientific ideas about sleep and dreaming are based on information derived from brain scans. *These very mechanistic theories tend to view the brain as little more than a machine, albeit a very complex one, and owe little if anything to Freud and his ideas about the unconscious mind and dreaming.*

* However, scientists have come up with intriguing new information that may again take us close to Freud. **Mark Solms**, a neurologist, has found that during REM sleep, areas of the brain responsible for the more complex thought processes are idle, while the so-called primitive areas involved with emotion and long-term memory are quite active.

* This suggested to Solms that dreams are not driven by REM sleep but by a

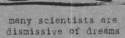

many scientists are dismissive of dreams

I had a great dream last night doc

work with brain-damaged people has supplied more evidence about dreaming

part of the brain that releases <u>DOPAMINE</u>. Solms submits work done with 26 patients who had lesions in the area of the brain that controls REM sleep as evidence for this. None of these patients could experience REM sleep, yet only one of them stopped dreaming. *However, a study of 350 patients with lesions in the frontal lobe area where dopamine neurons are located showed that all of them had stopped dreaming when the damage occurred.* According to Solms, the dopamine neurons stimulate the mind's "seeking" or "wanting" system, its motivational area—in short, its wishing system, which of course takes us back to Freud.

KEY WORDS

DOPAMINE:
A neurotransmitter that is active in the limbic system, the area of the brain that is involved in the regulation of emotion

SLEEP AND DREAMS IN CHILDREN

* Sleep in children is different from sleep in adults. Newborns sleep longer than older children and adults and spend more time in REM. Premature babies spend even longer periods asleep and have more REM sleep. The fetus in the womb spends most of its time asleep, and the majority of this sleep is REM sleep.

a child's dreaming is important for its growth

What do children dream about?

Although there are many instances of children dreaming of fairies and cuddly animals, most children will say they never have happy dreams. If you talk to children about their dreams, they will often tell you that they dream of being chased by hungry monsters, of witches and ghosts, and their dreams are generally full of anxieties and fears. Even when they dream about being the hero in an adventure, they are still very anxious in case they fail.

THE GROWING BRAIN

* All this would indicate that some sort of learning process is involved. After all, what would a fetus be dreaming about? REM sleep, during early stages of development at least, is involved with the growth of the brain. *We are born with about 100 billion brain cells. However, it is not the number of cells that matters, it is the connections between these cells. REM sleep seems to play an important part in establishing these connections.*

* The quantity of REM sleep decreases rapidly in the first few months of an infant's life, and by the age of 2 or 3 it takes up no more than about 25% of sleep time, not much different from that of an adult. It would be nice to think that an infant is living much of its life in a happy dream world. What is most likely is that and infant are in fact in an intense period of development of the cortex.

CHILDREN'S DREAMS

✱ At around age 3 or 4 children start to talk about dreaming. Prior to that they do not distinguish between waking and sleeping life, or between dreams and reality. *When they wake up they believe that the witch is still in the closet or the crocodile under the bed.*

there are no crocodiles in Arkansas, honey

children's dreams are often anxious

✱ *When children first describe dreams they do so in few words, probably because they do not remember much or are not completely sure that it was in fact a dream. At about age 5 or 6 they will talk freely about their dreams, and dreams at this age usually reflect the concerns of the day.*

AGGRESSION IN DREAMS

Boys between the ages of 4 and 12 are twice as likely as girls to report aggression in their dreams, and usually they themselves are the targets. During the early teen years it is reported by boys or girls equally, but by the age of 18 boys again report twice as many aggressive dreams as girls, although at 18 they are more likely to be the aggressor.

What do they think about their dreams?

Young children sometimes think dreams come from God or the fairies. Some children think dreams are for solving problems, for learning how to do things, and some think dreams give them a chance to practice what they might have to do during the day. Others think dreams are a kind of movie to keep them entertained while they are asleep.

23

NIGHTMARES

* It is not just children who have scary dreams. Anxiety is a common emotion in adult dreams also. A nightmare is a highly anxiety-laden dream that the dreamer remembers vividly for at least a short time after waking.

nightmares can be extremely alarming

nightmares are harmless

nightmares don't cause any lasting damage

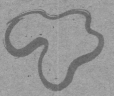

A PURSUER

* You are walking along a deserted country lane. You are aware that there is someone following you. You look behind, but cannot see anyone. If you speed up, the footsteps behind you also speed up. You try to run, but your legs just will not move the way they should; they seem to be moving in slow motion. Suddenly there is a hand on your shoulder. You try to scream; no sound comes… This is a classic nightmare.

"MARES"

* Nightmares are much more common in children than in adults. *They are dreams in which the dreamer feels helpless in the presence of danger and experiences overwhelming fear or anxiety.*

★ The Anglo-Saxon word <u>MARE</u> meant "demon" and was derived from the Sanskrit <u>MARA</u>, "destroyer," which in turn probably came from <u>MAR</u>, "to crush." Nightmares carry the connotation of horrific dreams of being crushed. *But nightmares are harmless—although if they are intense enough and frequent enough they can disturb sleep. Children who experience nightmares are unlikely to want to go to bed if they think they are going to be wakened by bad dreams.*

eat before you sleep
if you like

FOOD BEFORE BED

There is no truth in the old tale that eating certain foods—such as cheese—before you go to bed will give you nightmares, although going to bed soon after a large meal may well give you indigestion, which will disturb your sleep.

CAUSES OF NIGHTMARES

★ It is believed that people prone to nightmares have an exaggerated sensitivity. This may not manifest itself during the day but can appear at night in their dreams. *Nightmares can also be associated with different psychiatric conditions.* Obsessional patients, for example, will have nightmares of things getting out of control. Schizoid patients may well dream about being persecuted, devoured, or possessed. *Schizoid individuals generally keep themselves away from the group, and this can lead to a high degree of paranoid sensitivity, which will very likely come out in dreams.*

it's my exaggerated
sensitivity that
does it

some kinds of
mental illness
produce nightmares

25

help!!

NIGHT TERRORS

* During night terrors, as during sleepwalking, the mind appears to be only partially responsive to what is going on in the external world. Anxiety often seems to trigger these episodes. Many theories have been put forward to explain them and their underlying psychological meaning.

a loud scream is the first warning of a child's night terror

It has been suggested that, at least in adults, they are the expression of repressed emotional conflict that is deeply buried.

WORSE THAN A NIGHTMARE

* Night terrors are like nightmares, only worse. They can be distinguished from nightmares in two ways:

1. They do not occur in REM, or dream, sleep but in deep sleep.
2. People suffering night terrors have little or no memory of their content.

* Night terrors are much more common in children than in adults. One is usually alerted to the fact that a child is having a night terror by a horrific scream. You will usually find them sitting up in bed, staring. Their eyes are open

DISORIENTING

It can take up to 10 minutes to wake a child from a night terror, and during this period the child appears to be unaware of your existence. Even after waking up, the child may still be disoriented and it may take some time to calm him.

night terrors are mostly suffered by children

but they do not appear to be seeing anything. They are sweating, their heart is pounding, and if you try to hold them they struggle to get free.

NO MEMORY

✳ If you ask dreamers what they were dreaming about they usually cannot tell you, although adults will occasionally report feelings of dread and horror, sensations of being crushed. *Sometimes adults will report feelings of great shame, as though they had committed some crime. Most will have no memory of the incident the next day.*

Running in the family

Although night terrors can be quite common in young children, they do "grow out of them." They are rare in adolescents and even rarer in adults. Where night terrors persist into adulthood there is probably a genetic basis for this, because you will often find them in more than one member of the family.

Nightmares and night terrors demonstrate the difference between waking from two distinctly different stages of sleep. Waking from REM (the nightmare) you are almost immediately oriented to your surroundings. Waking from non-REM deep sleep (the night terror) there is disorientation and memory is limited.

someone who has had a
night terror will
probably not remember
it in the morning

27

so that is
the future

CHAPTER 2

INTEREST IN DREAMS

* Since earliest times people have seen dreams as the gateway to another world. Every culture and civilization with written language has left some trace or remnant of an interest in dreams and their meaning. There is a great deal of similarity in many of the beliefs about the meaning of dreams among different cultures.

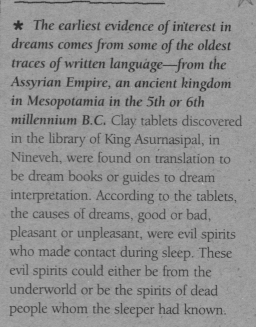

dreams were thought
to contain messages

was it really
evil then?

the Assyrians
thought dreams were
brought by evil
spirits

THE ASSYRIANS

* *The earliest evidence of interest in dreams comes from some of the oldest traces of written language—from the Assyrian Empire, an ancient kingdom in Mesopotamia in the 5th or 6th millennium B.C.* Clay tablets discovered in the library of King Asurnasipal, in Nineveh, were found on translation to be dream books or guides to dream interpretation. According to the tablets, the causes of dreams, good or bad, pleasant or unpleasant, were evil spirits who made contact during sleep. These evil spirits could either be from the underworld or be the spirits of dead people whom the sleeper had known.

THE EGYPTIANS

✱ The Egyptians believed that dreams were messages from the gods, and that they served three functions:

- **Advising the dreamer to repent for some offense, usually moral**
- **Warning of some danger in the future**
- **Answering questions that the dreamer had put to them**

✱ However, because dreams are seldom straightforward and because interaction between the gods and mortals could be risky, it was felt that dreams needed interpretation by experts to read between the lines and find the true message (not unlike today). *So the profession of dream interpreter was considered an honorable one, and practitioners were revered in their communities. They practiced in "serapea," temples of the Egyptian god of dreams.*

THE SAME DREAMS

The interesting thing about these early records is that they show that the content of dreams has not changed over thousands of years. The familiar mix of being chased, teeth falling out, as well as the bizarre sexual experiences that people report dreaming today were also dreamed by the Assyrians. And, just as in present-day accounts, they sometimes dreamed of finding themselves in the position of being naked in public.

INTERPRETERS

this is getting embarrassing

✱ The most famous serapea were in <u>MEMPHIS</u>, the Egyptian capital. Archaeologists in the 19th century uncovered a dream interpreter's room. Over the door was the inscription **"I interpret dreams, having the gods' mandate to do so. Good luck to you if you enter here."**

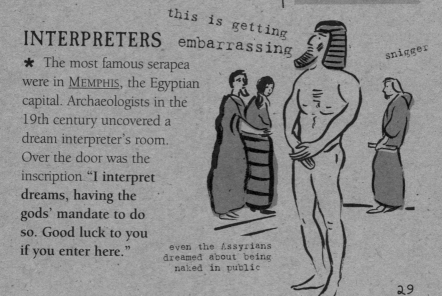

snigger

even the Assyrians
dreamed about being
naked in public

29

THE GREEKS

* The Greeks carried on the Egyptian practices in
the years before the birth of Christ. These
included the practice of incubation. Because the
gods would answer questions, put in a form advised
by dream interpreters, people with problems or
with mysteries to unravel would sleep in serapea
until the gods either answered their questions or
decided they were not worth bothering about.

INCUBATION

* Sometimes this would take several
nights. *The more important you were,
the more likely you were to have an
answer from the gods.* Royalty, for
example, generally had an answer on
the first night. It was considered that if
the gods had information that they
wanted passed on to a great number of
people they would do it through the
dreams of royalty. *So the dreams of kings
were deemed to be very important.*

royal dreams were
considered very
important

* The Greeks ascribed responsibility for
dreams to **Aesculapius**, the god of
healing. In the temples of Aesculapius the
role of incubation changed from general
advice to medical problems. *The god said
that when we dream our eyes turn inward
and light up our souls so that we can see
the truths hidden there, including truths
about our health. At the height of the
Greco-Roman era there were hundreds
of temples and many still exist.*

THE HEALING
SNAKE

Aesculapius, the Greek
god of healing, kept
snakes as his servants.
Today, the inter-
national symbol of
medical practitioners
is a serpent wound
around a staff, in
honor of Aesculapius.

in the temple of
Aesculapius the
dreamer would wait
for a healing dream

INSIDE THE TEMPLE OF AESCULAPIUS

✱ Initially, an animal would be slaughtered or gifts offered to the god. This ceremony was used to heighten awareness of the holiness of the occasion. *Suitably robed dreamers would enter the temple and lie down on a couch. The lights would then be dimmed and the supplicants would be left to await the visit of the god in their dreams.* If the supplicants had their dreams, hopefully containing good medical advice, they returned home the following morning. Otherwise, if they could afford it, they remained for another night or two.

✱ *It was believed that if a supplicant was very lucky Aesculapius himself or one of his attendants would visit in the dream, and if necessary would perform medical operations.*

BY INVITATION

If you wished to visit one of these temples you had to be invited by the gods in a dream. Those without such an invitation were unlikely to gain admittance. If you did have your story believed you would then have to submit to certain rituals. Bathing and sacrificial requirements were common, as were the requirements to abstain from alcohol and sex.

you got the invitation!

HYPNOS AND THANATOS

Sleep and death were often portrayed as being two sides of the same thing. The Greeks saw them as brothers: Hypnos, the god of sleep, and Thanatos, the god of death, were both sons of Nyx, the goddess of the night.

✱

31

HIPPOCRATES AND PLATO

* Hippocrates and Plato both believed in astrological influences on dream content. This is not as surprising as it may seem. Although both were highly intelligent men they also lived at a time when the stars were very important. People depended on the stars to guide their journeys across land and sea, and to tell them when to plant crops. Why should they not influence dreams?

Hippocrates believed the stars influenced our dreams

Hippocrates

HIPPOCRATES

* Hippocrates was a physician in the 5th century B.C. and is often known as the father of medicine because of his investigations. He was interested in what our dreams could tell us about impending disease. These dreams were called PRODROMAL, meaning "what has gone before." *He believed symptoms were delivered in dreams as symbols. For example, dreaming of rivers could be an indication of urological problems.*

* Hippocrates' theory may not be as preposterous as it sounds. There are many people today who claim to have prodromal dreams. Dreams giving insight into illness

have been chronicled by a number of modern writers. Hippocrates claimed that the sleeping brain, cut off from most influences of the outside world, gives increased importance to small signs that we are insensitive to during waking life. In the prodromal dream we are able to gain access to information that is already stored in the brain but hidden from us.

✱ Hippocrates also thought that dreams were divinely inspired—not surprisingly, because the gods were believed to take a close interest in human affairs—and he believed that astrological events could influence dreams.

Plato claimed that our dreams revealed the beast within

Plato

The philosopher Plato believed that since we have no control over our dreams we might find ourselves acting in them in ways we would not do while we were awake: things we might be too ashamed or embarrassed to do in other circumstances —"The virtuous man is prepared to dream what the wicked man really does." He also wrote that "even in good men there is a lawless wild beast nature which peers out in sleep" and he felt that all of our most forbidden wishes could be expressed in our dreams, thus predating some of the ideas of Freud and Jung by over 2,000 years.

Hippocrates said that dream symbols related to medical symptoms

33

ARISTOTLE

* Hippocrates, Plato, and Aristotle did not believe that we slept in order to dream. It was Plato's pupil Aristotle who first broke the link between the supernatural and dreaming. He felt that dreams had a physical source. His rejection of the psychic or divine origins of dreams was based on observation of animals, who he claimed had a dream life. This theory was established scientifically only in the middle of the twentieth century.

Aristotle

YOU DREAM WHAT YOU EAT

fumes from our food would gather in our heads and give us dreams, said Aristotle.

* Aristotle considered that the immediate cause of sleep is the food that we eat. *This food would give off fumes into the veins, and the heat of the body would drive these fumes into the head where they would collect and cause sleep. This sleep would last until all the food had been digested.* This, he explained, is why we so often have fits of drowsiness after eating meals.

* Aristotle also tried to explain children's need for extra sleep in the same terms. Hyperactivity leads to the same "fumes" in the head as eating, thus

Aristotle recognized a connection between our dreams and the waking world

Ancient and modern ideas

Ancient theories of dreams and dreaming may seem outlandish to us today, but some do in fact foreshadow modern theories—such as the restorative nature of sleep and the therapeutic value of understanding our dreams.

causing the need for sleep. This also explains why the child's head is disproportionately large for its body.

✴ *Aristotle did believe we dream—indeed, he wrote three books on dreaming. He did not, however, believe that dreams were sent by the gods. He believed that they were the mental activity of the sleeper. He was aware of the fact that in dreams we sometimes magnify small changes in the external world—for example dreaming we are in a fire when in reality we have too many blankets—and he felt that dreams could be a way for our mind to tell us all is not well with our bodies. Thus dreams could be an early manifestation of illness of which the waking mind is as yet unaware.*

ARE DREAMS REAL OR IMAGINED?

When we look at the dream beliefs of early civilizations and other cultures find both similarities and differences in the way that people regard their dreams. But we find a fairly universal unquestioning belief that dreams are real experiences. Whether they are interactions with the gods or devils, or travels in some other spiritual world, they are not imaginings, they are real.

EASTERN APPROACHES TO DREAMING

* It was not just the Mediterranean civilizations that believed in the dynamic features of dreaming. All cultures appear to believe that while dreams occur in a self-contained world of their own, there is a paradoxical nature to them—of this world and yet not of it.

ancient Indians believed dreaming to be a place between this world and another

INDIA

* The VEDAS, the sacred books of Indian wisdom, which were written about 1500–1000 B.C., classify dreams as lucky and unlucky. They were interested in what dreams can predict. The last dream in a series of dreams is the most important to the dreamer, and the later in the night it comes the more likely it is to come true. *The temperament of the dreamer was linked to the content of the dream: Depressed people had depressed dreams and happy people had happy dreams.*

LEVELS OF CONSCIOUSNESS

* One of the interesting features of the Vedas is that they understand dreaming

YOGA

There are 8 states in traditional yoga. The first two deal with calming desires and emotions. The next 2 deal with the reduction of movement, internal and external. The fifth deals with detachment from what is going on around you. The sixth and seventh deal with concentration on a fixed object, and further detachment. And in the final stage there is "absorption," in which state the yogi is said to gain paranormal powers.

as a different LEVEL OF CONSCIOUSNESS. They say that there are two states, one in this world and one in the other, and that there is an intermediate place between the two that is dreaming. In dreaming the soul leaves the body and, protected by the sleeper's breath, floats between this world and the other world, and from there can perceive both.

✱ *The waking state was considered less real than the dream state, because the dream state has access to both the realm of knowledge and the realm of experience. The highest state is that of transcending beyond dreams to a dreamless sleep where, untroubled by worldly preoccupations, we are at one with infinity. Trance techniques such as yoga are used for the inducement of this state of bliss.*

SLEEP AND DEATH

The difference between sleep and death, as still considered in some cultures, is that the soul returns to the body of the sleeper before he or she wakes up. The Chinese believed in two kinds of soul. A material soul, P'o, was said to be the physical essence of the person and died with them. A spiritual soul, Hun, could leave the body every night during sleep and departed for the spirit world at the moment of death.

CHINA

✱ The paradoxical nature of dreaming was noted by the early Chinese dream writers. But they also saw dreams as offering information culled from another world, which could be used to our advantage in this world. *Free to leave the body, the soul could communicate with gods and spirits and learn from them. These experiences were treated with great reverence, and the Chinese, like the Greeks, also practiced incubation.*

the Chinese treated dreams with great reverence

dream about
devilish thing

EUROPE BEFORE THE FREUDIAN REVOLUTION

* Europe in the Middle Ages was a very superstitious place and the devil was seen as a strong character waiting to pounce at the first sign of weakness.

in the Middle Ages it was feared that the devil controlled your dreams

Everyone had to be constantly alert. It is not surprising, therefore, that in medieval times dreams were viewed with much suspicion, being the prime place for the devil to strike.

JOAN OF ARC

Joan believed that she was inspired by God to liberate France from the English. She believed that she received her messages from God in her dreams through saints and angels. She also communicated with them while awake, heard their voices, and claimed she could see and touch them. The authorities believed these messages came from the devil and Joan was burned at the stake as a witch.

HEAVEN-SENT OR DEVIL-SENT DREAMS?

* In Europe during the Middle Ages dreams were seen as evil, and with the religious obsessions that built up around the time of the REFORMATION, this idea of the evil nature of dreams continued to grow. It was generally believed that though one could have messages from God or the saints, most dreams were demonically induced.

* Joan of Arc was believed to get her dreams or visions from demonic sources, though she thought they were from God. Most people in fact were suspicious of alleged dreams from God or the saints, because the devil was known to have great powers of deception and it was believed

that he could infiltrate dreams and plant ideas in disguise. *Martin Luther was plagued with ambiguous dreams, and he prayed to be spared any messages from God in case they should be confused with messages from the devil.*

my dreams come from God

Luther did not trust his dreams

Joan of Arc was inspired by her dreams to liberate France

The Romantics

With the advent of the Romantic era the link was made between the unconscious and dreaming. The Romantics believed that the unconscious was an expression of nature and therefore the source of all creativity and imagination, which could be seen in art, poetry, madness, and dreams (something we will look at later in this book). This led to the more enlightened theorizing of the 19th and 20th centuries and to the writings of Sigmund Freud and Carl Jung.

* *With the dawn of the Age of Reason, and the increasing interest in the anatomy of the body and brain, physical theories began to replace metaphysical ones.* By the 17th century the philosopher Thomas Hobbes was able to declare that dreams were due to a distemper of what he called "the inward parts."

enlightened
thinker

Freud

39

FREUD AND JUNG

✱ In the period between the Middle Ages and Freud, many theorists tried to explain the nature of dreams. Dreams were linked to digestion and the "flowing of bodily juices" in one direction or another, or to physiology in some other way. There were also those who believed that dreams were products of mind and memory, and even some who saw the symbolism of dreams as important. However, it was Freud who developed the most important and far-reaching theory of dreams ever written.

no physical cause

many of Freud's patients exhibited symptoms that had no physical cause

TWO KINDS OF REALITY

Freud suggested that there were two kinds of reality: an objective reality, which is the external world, that is seen by everyone; and a psychological or internal reality that is perceived only by the self

EMOTIONAL ILLNESS

✱ **Sigmund Freud** (1856–1939) was born in Freiburg, Moravia. He went to Vienna to study medicine. In the early days of his clinical practice, Freud was intrigued by the observation that many of his patients exhibited symptoms that had no physical cause, such as blindness or paralysis, delusions or hallucinations. *He began to believe that the cause of these conditions was emotional, a feeling that grew into a conviction when he found that by allowing patients to talk freely about their problems, the symptoms often disappeared.*

✱ This appeared to be particularly true when forgotten traumatic events in childhood, and the feelings that went with them, were brought to light. Many of these memories were of a sexual or aggressive nature, and Freud believed that they had been thrust out of conscious

Freud's work led to the development of psychoanalysis

awareness because they were too painful or shameful to think about. Freud found that middle-class women among his patients revealed powerful sexual emotions that had links with childhood. And many of these emotions were manifest in their dreams.

SCANDAL

✱ Freud's findings were greeted with horror. The ideas he was putting forward were very threatening to 19th-century society. He was questioning the sexual role of women in society, a society that wanted to deny that role altogether, and implying that children were capable of sexual feeling, even if only a rudimentary kind. *The theory of infantile sexuality that grew out of this is widely accepted today, but then it was seen as a heresy.*

PSYCHOANALYSIS

Psychoanalysis grew out of this early work of Freud's. Allowing patients to "free associate," to give rein to whatever comes to mind without editing or censoring, sometimes brings conflicts—repressed emotions and motives—into awareness. The goal of psychoanalysis is to deal with these conflicts in a more rational and realistic way. Freud has been criticized by some modern psychologists as being too conservative in his views, especially his views of women. But we have to remember that Freud was formulating his theories in the 1890s, a time much different from today, and that to some extent, Freud was a man of his time. But he was also a man of courage and belief in his ideas.

CONSCIOUS AND UNCONSCIOUS

✻ Freud was suggesting that unconscious mental processes were significant in determining human behavior, another notion that went against the thinking of the time. He was shunned by the scientific establishment and many of his patients rejected him. But Freud persisted, and his lifelong search into the nature of the human mind has gone into history.

sweet dreams
are made
of this...

Freud claimed that dreams reflect our unconscious desires

WISH FULFILLMENT

✻ Freud proposed that the function of dreams is to REGULATE or adjust the effect of the sleeper's experiences so that he or she can continue sleeping. *He believed that the conflict between forbidden sexual desires and the repression of those desires through fear of the consequences produces a tension in the personality. This tension discharges itself during the dream.* The purpose of the dream is, therefore, to relieve this tension by gratifying the wish and so allowing the individual to sleep.

★ Freud suggested that the dream is the protector of sleep; one dreams in order to continue sleeping.

Freud suggests that the
dream is the protector
of sleep

JUNG

★ One of Freud's closest and most influential followers, **Carl Jung** (1875–1961) seems from the very beginning to have regarded dreams as creation, messages from some agent, but he seems also to have had some difficulty in deciding who or what this agent might be, or in finding a satisfactory way of referring to him, her, or it. Hence such statements as "The dream is a mysterious message from our night aspect" and "One does not dream, one is dreamed. We undergo the dreams, we are the objects." But he leaves the composer of the message unnamed. This was a very different attitude to dreams than that held by Freud.

★ *Jung believed that every dream was so individual that there could be no systematic interpretation of dreams. Every dream must be looked at with the dreamer because the dreamer would have insights that were denied by the conscious mind.*

Jung vs. Freud

*The difference between Jung and Freud is that Jung regarded dreams as manifestations and creations not only of the person dreaming but also of something called the **collective unconscious**. In Jung's view the agent who sends messages in dreams is both a person and the collective impersonal, a part of oneself which one shares with others. Jung also seems to have believed that we dream continuously, even when awake: "It is on the whole probable that we continually dream, but that consciousness makes such a noise that we do not hear."*

KEY WORDS

COLLECTIVE UNCONSCIOUS: This is a term used by Jung to describe those elements in the individual's unconscious derived from the experience of the race.

THE BRAIN AS A MACHINE

✱ Although the psychoanalytic tradition of dream interpretation still continues, with new ways of looking at sleep and particularly REM, or dream, sleep, new theories have emerged that reject the psychological view of dreams, preferring to see the dreaming brain as a kind of machine.

I'm not dreaming well now

really

are dreams a way of cleaning up our internal computer?

THE NEED TO DREAM

Evans and Newman believe that if the dream processing is interrupted and there is a prolonged deprivation of dreaming or the opportunity to dream, then this will produce a breakdown in human efficiency. Could this be seen perhaps as the modern equivalent of the soul not getting back into the body?

BRAINS AS COMPUTERS

✱ Two British computer scientists, **Christopher Evans** and **Ted Newman**, propose a theory using an analogy from computers. They suggest that the dream process has the same function as the systematic program clearance that is necessary when computer programs evolve to meet changing circumstances. *The greater the change, the greater must be the amount of program evolution, and the more urgent the program clearing.*

COMPUTER SLEEP

✱ *In their view, the primary function of sleep is probably to allow such a clearing process to get under way without interference from external information. Dreams occur when the level of consciousness shifts for one reason or another and the clearing process is interrupted. They believe that sleep is a period when the brain disengages from the external world and uses this off-line time to reorganize the vast array of information that was put in during the day.*

✱ According to Evans, the brain is like a computer with large data banks and an assortment of control programs. Sleep, particularly REM sleep, occurs when the brain comes off line, isolating itself from the body. *In this off-line period various data banks and files are opened and become available for a reorganization based on the experiences of the day.* In the language of computer science, this process is an <u>INTERLOCKING PROCEDURE</u>, in which computer instructions are not erased, but new ones are added instead.

From A to B

In this theory there are two kinds of dreams. **Type A** *dreams are the full array of off-line processing that occurs during REM sleep—we are not aware of this process.* **Type B** *dreams are nothing more than the small segments of type A, which we remember if we are awakened during REM sleep. The brain comes back on line and the conscious mind observes a small sample of the program being run.*

according to some
scientists, dreaming
is like filing

THE TRASH-CAN THEORY OF DREAMS

* The machine analogy of the brain was continued by other writers. In the 1980s, when there was a great deal of interest in neural networks, a theory emerged linking these with dreams.

too many bugs can confuse the brain

it needs **debugging**

human brain

Crick claimed that our brains can get overloaded

IN THE CAN

It would appear that Crick believed that dreams are little more than random noise with no content. It has been suggested, perhaps a mite unkindly, that had this theory been proposed by someone less exalted than a Nobel Laureate, it might have ended up in the garbage can!

Crick's theory?

the theory narrowly missed the garbage can

A NEW THEORY

* In 1983, **Francis Crick**, the Nobel Laureate, and **Graeme Mitchison**, building on the theory of Evans, proposed a theory of dreaming based on a model of the brain that is a NEURAL NETWORK. *This is a network where when one neuron fires, it excites other neurons around it and they fire in turn, or at the same time.* Crick believed that this kind of system is likely to be subject to unwanted "parasitic modes of behavior," and proposed that these behaviors need to be cleared out, and that they are detected and suppressed by some kind of mechanism, which operates during REM sleep.

UNLEARNING

✱ This process is the opposite of learning: Instead it is <u>REVERSE LEARNING</u> or <u>UNLEARNING</u>. Crick claimed that this system of unlearning is not the same as forgetting, and suggested that too many memories in one network may produce either bizarre associations or the same response whatever kind of stimulus is triggered. *To deal with this information overload, he suggested that the brain needs a mechanism to debug and tune the network, and that such a debugging mechanism would work best when the system was isolated from the external world and would have a way of randomly zapping the network, in order to get rid of these spurious connections.* He further suggested that the hallucinatory quality of dreams is nothing more than the random firing needed for this daily cleanup of the network.

now class we will unlearn yesterday's geography lesson

Forget everything

Crick thought that trying to remember one's dreams may not be a good idea. Such remembering could help to retain patterns of thought that are best forgotten, the very patterns that the system is trying to get rid of.

I'm reverse learning spanish tonight

some thought patterns need to be removed to make room

47

ding ding
dong

CHAPTER 3
LUCID DREAMING

* In a lucid dream the dreamer is aware that he is dreaming and has some control over the dream. He also appears to be very aware of the dreaming environment and to have some memory of his waking life. Some describe these dreams as being completely realistic, and the dreamers will say they feel very much like their normal selves.

there's another
one for the
collection

WHO DREAMS LUCID DREAMS?

sleep researchers
collect examples
of dreams

* When I first started collecting dreams in a sleep laboratory, I was very surprised to find that some people appeared to have some control over their dreams, over how the dream story unfolds. *I was further surprised to find that many people report having this ability to a greater or lesser degree.* Few people have such dreams regularly, at least not every night, but many report having them from time to time.

* *All who do describe the same kind of sensations. They know they are dreaming and*

noisy Lucid Dreams
clock

they are aware that they have some control over their actions in the dream, even to the extent of changing the ending of the dream because they did not like the first one.

✱ There are, alas, people like myself who have never experienced a lucid dream; try as I might, I have been unable to change that. Yet many report

Hervey de St. Denys was one of the first lucid dreamers

that it is a technique that can be learned. However, Peter Fenwick, who has carried out research in this area, suggests that unless you are a "natural," it may take a very long time to learn. *He cites Saint-Denys, an early lucid dreamer, as having tried for 207 nights before his first lucid dream. The second came on night 214. At the end of 6 months he was having about 2 per week.*

GOOD FUN

✱ Those who do have lucid dreams say it is an exhilarating experience, and it is worth persisting in trying to learn. Peter Fenwick describes it as being the closest that human beings can get to a FANTASY LIFE that is virtual reality. He says it is as if you are conscious even though you are asleep. You can think and reason, make decisions and act on them, all the time aware that you are in a dream world, which gives a wonderful sense of freedom.

AN EARLY LUCID DREAM

In 1867 the Marquis Hervey de Saint-Denys recorded that the striking of a nearby clock was incorporated into his dream. He recognized it for what it was, a noisy clock near his house in Paris, and knew he was dreaming. He was able to work out what the time was and how much time he had left before he had to wake up.

I knew I was dreaming

Van Eeden

Van Eeden's dream experiment

Van Eeden decided to see if he could carry out an experiment in a dream. He dreamed: "I stood at a table before a window. On the table were different objects. I was perfectly aware I was dreaming and considered what kind of experiments I could make. I took a glass from the table and struck it with my fist with all my might, reflecting while I was doing it how dangerous this would be to do in waking life. The glass remained whole. But lo! When I look at it again some time later it is broken. I then proceeded to throw the broken glass out of the window to discover whether I could hear it tinkle on the cobbles below. I heard the noise all right and even saw two dogs running away from it quite naturally. But I thought what a good imitation this comedy world was."

SO WHAT IS GOING ON IN LUCID DREAMS?

* The term was first used by Dutch psychiatrist Fredrick Willelms van Eeden in a paper he gave in London in 1913. Having started at age 13, he had recorded 352 lucid dreams over a period of 14 years. What had interested van Eeden was that he was not only conscious that he was dreaming but able to carry out acts of free will during his dreams.

van Eeden decided to break a glass in his dream

now

there have been
experiments to test
lucid dreaming

BEATING THE SKEPTICS

* People have generally dismissed lucid
dreams as fantasy. *But with better techniques
for looking at sleep and more interest in the
scientific study of dreaming, it has become
apparent that there is another different and
quite distinct kind of dream out there.*

* Research into lucid dreams has
shown that the dreamers really are aware
that they are dreaming. There is usually a
recognition of some kind of dreamlike
quality in what otherwise seems very
much like waking life. It may be noticing
an inconsistency, such as having a
conversation with someone who is dead.
*Once the dreamer has come to the
conclusion that they are dreaming, they
often test it out by changing the course
of action in the dream, or sometimes by
deciding to fly.*

DREAM MACHINES

Several dream workers
have tried to develop
machines to induce
lucid dreams. Because
lucid dreams occur in a
light phase of sleep,
the machine tries to
detect (usually with
pressure pads on the
eyes) when a sleeper is
in REM sleep, and
then to partially awaken
them so that they enter
a lighter stage of sleep
without waking up.
They are then given
external cues such as
voices or flashing
lights in the hope that
a lucid dream will
develop. Such
machines have not been
very successful; sleepers
usually either wake up
or go back to REM
sleep.

it's all fantasy

51

DREAM CONSCIOUSNESS

Omm

* People who have lucid dreams realize they are dreaming during an ongoing dream. But what Peter Fenwick calls "dream consciousness" can begin in wakefulness. Through this method one can create lucidity on demand. Stephen Le Berg at the Stanford University Sleep Center believes he can use lucid dreams for a variety of

Tibetan yogis practice dream consciousness

purposes. By training himself to remain conscious he claims he can ask characters in his dreams for advice, conquer his enemies, and bring about happy endings that make him feel more self-confident.

CAN ONE REALLY LEARN TO DREAM LUCIDLY?

* Le Berg claims to have taught himself and many of his students how to become proficient lucid dreamers. He has also pioneered ways of enabling subjects to indicate when they become aware of dreaming in their sleep. They do this by rapidly moving their eyes vertically. This has led to several interesting findings about dreams, such as the

I love a happy ending

if your dream is sad, you can change the ending

fact that time estimation in dreams corresponds to real time. **What takes 5 minutes in a dream would take 5 minutes in reality.** If we seem to move rapidly from one distant area to another in a dream it is because we don't dream about the actual traveling itself.

it only took 5 minutes to dream it

you can get advice from someone in your dream

WHY LEARN LUCID DREAMING?

✷ Lucid dreams can be emotionally beneficial. *We can conquer our fears in our dreams, but most ordinary dreams have some anxiety or sadness in them.* Reports of lucid dreams rarely contain negative emotions: When unpleasant emotion intrudes, the dreamers can change it into something more enjoyable, because they know "this is only a dream and nothing to worry about."

CONSCIOUSNESS IN SLEEP

The ability to maintain waking consciousness while falling asleep has been practiced by Tibetan Yogis since the 8th century, and is seen as the gateway to mystic states. The yogis believe that knowledge perceived by the senses in either the waking or sleeping state is equally unreal. Masters of Tibetan yoga are said to be able to pass in and out of sleep without ever losing consciousness. Using meditation techniques, the ability to maintain consciousness in dream sleep has also been practiced in India for many centuries.

LEARNING TO DREAM LUCIDLY

* A number of authors have suggested techniques to learn lucid dreaming. Begin by questioning yourself during the day. Am I awake? Am I asleep? Is this a dream? Is this wakefulness? Do this as often as possible. Try to remember all of your dreams even if they are not lucid. When you wake from a dream try to remember every detail of it before doing anything else. Tell yourself that the next dream will be one in which you will be aware you are dreaming. Remind yourself that you are about to have a lucid dream. Many people report success with these methods.

set your alarm so that you only sleep for 3 or 4 hours

CONTROLLING YOUR LUCID DREAMS

Lucid dreams do not give a person a clean slate to decide what to dream. Dreamers can control the course and, to some extent, the content of the dream, but they have to accept its basic scenario, wherever they find themselves.

SET YOUR CLOCK

* Peter Fenwick suggests that to improve your chances of having a lucid dream, set your alarm so that you only sleep for 3 or 4 hours. Then stay awake until your normal time for getting up. Then let yourself go back to sleep. This time you are more likely to have dream sleep and thus a lucid dream.

there are ways to improve your chance of having a lucid dream

LUCID NAPS

* Fenwick suggests that as the afternoon is a higher point in the alertness cycle you are less likely to fall asleep too deeply and are therefore more likely to have lucid dreams. One to try at your desk, perhaps?

the afternoon is a good time for lucid dreams

* Other researchers suggest testing the reality of your surroundings during the day to see if you are awake or asleep. *Is anything surreal about your world? Can you pass through walls, for example? Try to switch a light on or off, or read a newspaper. (Both these tasks are reported to be very difficult to do in lucid dreams.)* The suggestion is that if someone habitually carries out these checks during the day, they will find themselves doing the same thing during their dreams, and perhaps stumble on lucidity, which they can then test.

* Another idea is to find a friend who also wants to have a lucid dream, and agree to meet in your dream in a specific place that you both know well. **If possible make it a place that you both see every day in waking consciousness.** During the day, every time you see this place remind yourself that you are going to meet your friend there in your dream, and think about it before you go to sleep. This works for some people.

FALSE DAWNS

One of the interesting things that lucid dreamers report is false awakenings in which the dreamer "awakens" into another dream. One woman reported that she awoke from a lucid dream, got up and got dressed, had her breakfast, and left for work. She then woke up realizing it had been a dream, got dressed, had breakfast, and left for work. This happened again for a third time before she finally and actually got up.

CHAPTER 4
THE CREATIVE DREAM

* The very act of dreaming is a creative act. We take memories of what we have done or worried over the day before, we take memories of our childhood, and perhaps unresolved conflicts, into our dreams and weave a story around them which, at least for the duration of the dream, will make some sense. For many of us these stories will have some relevance to our waking lives.

A PROBLEM

The Stanford sleep researcher Dement gave this puzzle to 500 students to work on. Write down the following letters on a piece of paper and put it by your bed. H, I, J, K, L, M, N, O. For a few minutes before you go to sleep look at them and think what they might mean. You are looking for a single word answer! The solution is on page 59.

dreams are creative

I designed it in my sleep

SLEEP ON IT

* Many people report that the old adage about sleeping on a problem is a very useful one. Studies show that people faced with a demanding situation such as a job interview will spend more of the night in REM sleep. A group of recently divorced women who were depressed and a group who were not depressed were studied, and it was found that the depressed women needed considerably more dream time. It may be that those who have suffered stress use dreams to accelerate readjustment into their new situation

USING OUR DREAMS

✱ *It is not just to enhance our emotional life that our dreams can help us; it would appear that they can also help enhance our intellectual performance. It has been shown that there is correlation between the amount of REM sleep and memory. The more you dream, the better your memory becomes.*

I'm enhancing my intellectual performance with night classes

sleeping on a problem really can help solve it

Testing the power of dreams

Can we use our dreams for problem solving? In 1983, Morton Schatzman decided to put this to the test. In an article in the London Sunday Times *he posed a problem that he asked readers to solve.*
What is curious about this sentence?
Show this bold Prussian that praises slaughter, slaughter brings rout.
He suggested that people think about this when they are falling asleep, and write down any dreams they remember on awakening. He hoped that readers would write to him with the solution. On the next two pages we reveal what happened.

SLEEPING ON THE PROBLEM

✳ Schatzman had fewer responses to his article than he expected. Some people responded with what they thought was the answer, answers that made sense to them, but unfortunately did not solve the puzzle. However, there were some who got parts of it, or came close to the answer, indicating that their minds were wrestling with the problem while they were asleep.

COMPUTER ROOM

my name is
Michael Caine

A complex process

This story illustrates the complexity of our thinking processes while we are dreaming. All the clues were revealed in the dream, the guillotine to suggest beheading or lopping off, laughter ringing out, the Sunday Times *under Michael Caine's arm. Of course, it is possible that the solution was already pre-consciously known to the dreamer, and these clues were just pointers to it.*

HELP FROM A SPY

✳ After a few days, one person sent the following dream to Schatzman. She had gone to bed memorizing the puzzle but not really expecting to solve it.

✳ *"I'm watching Michael Caine in one of his spy roles, possibly the Ipcress File. He's in the center, or whatever spy headquarters are called. He walks up to a door marked 'Computer Room' and opens it. Behind the door is a heavy wire-mesh screen. He passes a folded copy of the* Sunday Times *to someone behind the screen.*

✳ *"From the computer room come sounds of whining tapes and other computer type noises. I see that through a slot in the screen is being pushed a colored comic postcard with a caption at* the bottom. Michael Caine takes it, looks at it, chuckles briefly, and hands it to me.

✱ "The postcard comes to life and I'm sitting in an audience watching a stage show. On the stage, a comic figure in doublet and hose, wearing a hat with an enormous feather, is kneeling with his head in a guillotine. He looks apprehensively at the audience and rolls his eyes. The audience rocks with laughter and the comic figure struggles to his feet, comes to the front of the stage and says, 'Sh-sh-sh! Laughter is a capital offense.' More laughter from the audience. The comic figure doffs his hat in an extravagant manner and bows.

✱ "For some reason I feel very grateful to Michael Caine and turn to thank him. He says nothing but points over his shoulder to indicate that he must dash, and with a friendly wave walks off."

✱ When the dreamer woke up at the end of the dream, she turned on the light, looked at the problem in the *Sunday Times* and found she knew the answer. The first letter of each word could be lopped off to reveal the solution: *How his old Russian hat raises laughter, laughter rings out.*

the answer was in the dream

ANSWER TO PUZZLE ON PAGE 57

The word is Water. The letters H, I, J, K, L, M, N, O = H to O, H_2O.

how his old Russian hat raises laughter, laughter rings out.

PROBLEM-SOLVING DREAMS

* There are many instances in science and literature where breakthrough ideas have been revealed in a dream. However, most of these have come not as a bolt out of the blue, but rather as the response to a long period of wrestling with a problem.

MAKING THE CONNECTION

* The preconscious mind will have been searching for a solution although the conscious mind is unaware of this. *So the creative insights that result will have come from a reorganization of information already held in the memory.* In our dreams

Kekule discovered the structure of benzene in a dream

BENZENE DREAMS

One of the most famous breakthroughs in science came from an afternoon nap. The chemist Friedrich Kekule (1829–96) had for some years been struggling with the problem of solving the molecular structure of benzene. He relates that he fell asleep and saw, as he had seen many times before, atoms dancing before his eyes. He saw a chain of carbon and hydrogen atoms twisting and turning in a snakelike motion. Suddenly one of these "snakes" bit its own tail and whirled before him. He woke with a start— he had solved the problem. Carbon compounds like benzene, he realized, were not open structures but were closed chains: snakes biting their tails.

we scan our memory stores in an attempt to find past experiences that correspond in some way to our present dilemmas. **The creativity comes from making seemingly unrelated connections relevant.**

improved swing

even golf can benefit from dreaming

CREATIVE DREAMS IN SCIENCE

✱ The inventor of the sewing machine, Elias Howe, had been struggling for some time for a way of mechanizing the sewing process. One night

a sewing machine

he had a nightmare in which he was taken captive by a hostile tribe, who told him "Either produce a machine that sews in the 24 four hours or die." In his dream, as in his waking life, he was unable to deliver the machine. His captors gathered around him with spears poised ready to kill him. As the spears descended he noticed that there were eye-shaped holes in the tips of the spears. He awoke, in a sweat, before the weapons plunged into his body.

✱ *As he lay there trembling, remembering his dream, he remembered those oddly placed holes and realized that if he were to put a hole in such a position on his sewing needle, his idea for mechanization might just work. This dream led to the revolution of the clothing industry.*

A DREAM SWING

In an interview in the *San Francisco Chronicle* in 1964 the golfer Jack Nicklaus described how, during a low point in his career when couldn't improve his game, he dreamed that he was holding his club differently and swinging perfectly. When he got to the course the next morning he tried holding his club the way he had in his dream; it worked perfectly and his game improved.

Coleridge

KUBLA KHAN

✴ It is not just in science that creative dreams have been the source of inspiration. Possibly the best known of dream-inspired creations is Samuel Taylor Coleridge's narrative poem *Kubla Khan*.

NOT PROVEN

Some doubts have been expressed about a dream's being the genesis of this famous poem. Coleridge claimed that it was an act of spontaneous creation; however, in 1934 an autograph copy of the manuscript of *Kubla Khan* was discovered, and it showed that there had been several earlier drafts written before publication. But this does not mean that we should dismiss the story of the creation of *Kubla Khan* out of hand. It is most likely that Coleridge exaggerated the spontaneity of the writing, rather than fabricated the story of the dream.

IN THE COUNTRY

✴ In the summer of 1797, Coleridge was staying at a lonely farmhouse near Porlock in Devon. As he describes it in the preface to the poem, he had been prescribed an "anodyne for a slight indisposition." This anodyne was opium, and he fell into an opium-induced sleep while reading the following account in a history book: **"Here the Khan Kubla commanded a palace to be built and a stately garden thereunto. And thus 10 miles of fertile ground were enclosed with a wall."**

✴ Coleridge describes how in his subsequent dream he **"could not have composed less than 200 to 300 lines… in which all the images rose up before him as things."** He goes on to describe the clarity and realism of the dream images, which interlocked to form a coherent story **"without any sensation or conscious effort."** On waking, Coleridge began to write down his dream poem, which begins:

In Xanadu did Kubla Khan
A stately pleasure dome decree
Where Alph, the sacred river, ran
Through caverns measureless to man
Down to a sunless sea.

✱ Alas, he was interrupted in his writing by the visit of the infamous "person on business from Porlock," who detained him for an hour. When he returned to his room he found that although he retained a faint memory of the dream, and some scattered sharp images, the rest of the dream had evaporated. *And so what was left was still a magnificent poem, but a poem of 53 lines rather than 200 to 300 lines.*

William Blake was a firm believer in the creative power of dreams

William Blake

Many authors have cited their sleeping life as the source of some of their best creations. The poet and painter **William Blake** *(1757–1827) cited dreams as a creative source. He believed that he received visitations from the spirit world in his dreams. Blake even made a drawing called "The Man who Taught Blake Painting in his Dreams."*

In Xanadu did Kubla Khan

Coleridge wrote Kubla Khan in a drug-induced reverie

do an E seventh next

the devil was supposed to have dictated a tune to Guiseppe Tartini in his dreams

DREAMS AS INSPIRATION

* We are all authors. Every night our mind takes the happenings and thoughts of the day before, and weaves them together with images from our memory, making stories that can be grotesque or sublime. They can entertain or frighten, they can remind us of past events we have forgotten, and sometimes they even solve our problems.

Artistic vision

It must be remembered that dreams come largely from memory, and it is unlikely that someone who has never written or painted before will suddenly wake up one morning and re-create a masterpiece from a dream. The necessary skill and craft must already be there in the artist for them to carry this out.

TURNING DREAMS INTO BOOKS

* The majority of us leave matters there. We do not actually turn our dreams into a salable commodity. But some writers claim that their best and most creative ideas come from their dreams. **Mary Shelley** based *Frankenstein* on a dream. The writer **Robert Louis Stevenson** turned

Mary Shelley

a dream about leading a double life into his famous story of Doctor Jekyll and Mister Hyde. Stevenson used many of his dreams as the basis for his stories. *He claimed to be able to dream complete narratives on a regular basis, and to pick up on subsequent nights the dream story that had started the night before. He was dreaming his books episode by episode!* He came to rely on his dreams for ideas for his stories, and called them his "Brownies or Little People" who "…God bless them, do half my work for me when I am asleep."

DREAMS TO THE RESCUE

✱ **Voltaire** and **Goethe** also claimed to have had poems come to them in dreams, and the novelist **Graham Greene** didn't just dream his stories and characters, but dreamed his characters' dreams. He describes how when he was writing *A Burnt Out Case* he had a dream. *The symbols, memories, and associations of the dream struck Greene as belonging so clearly to his main character, Quarry, that the next morning he was able to put the dream, without changing it, into the novel, where it solved a problem with the narrative that he had been grappling with for many days.*

✱ This illustrates the integration of the inspirational and problem-solving nature of dreams, and the creativity of the artist in using them in a productive way.

Goethe

THE DEVIL HAS ALL THE BEST TUNES

The Italian composer Guiseppe Tartini had a dream in which the devil appeared to him and offered that in return for Tartini's soul he would teach him to compose the most beautiful music in the world. He took Tartini's violin and began to play a piece of such exquisite beauty that Tartini was moved to tears. When he woke he tried to reproduce the sound. The piece he wrote, "The Devil's Trill," is a beautiful piece of music and the composer felt it was best he had ever written, but he describes it as faint and remote from what he heard in his dream.

65

CHAPTER 5

THE ROAD TO DREAM INTERPRETATION

* Dreams occur 4 or 5 times every night. Over the average life span we spend about a third of our lives asleep, and approximately 5 years of that time dreaming!

we spend about 5 years of our life dreaming

And yet, despite the existence of so many theories about dreams and how to interpret them, this remarkable state remains mysterious. No one truly knows why we dream, or what dreams mean.

DEVIL'S WORK

* Over the centuries dreams have become associated with the PARANORMAL, and the occurrence of unusual events, such as leaving the body, being visited by an incubus, or predicting future events. *Saint Jerome said that interpreting dreams was akin to witchcraft, and within two centuries the practice was forbidden to members of the Christian church.*

* The first sign of change was when **Descartes** developed his philosophy, but real change came when **Freud** wrote his classic book *The Interpretation of Dreams*, which defined dreams as psychological not religious events, and dream interpretation became more acceptable.

the first sign of change was when Descartes developed his philosophy

KEY WORDS

SLEEP PARALYSIS: An inability to move upon waking, sometimes accompanied by hallucinations and fear.

DEMONIC VISITATIONS

✳ Sleep involves varying levels of consciousness. Sometimes stages overlap and people can think that they are awake when they are actually still asleep. This STATE-CONFUSION has recently been suggested as the cause of many "paranormal phenomena," like seeing ghosts or aliens at the foot of the bed.

hello

all the nuns thought they were visited by a demon

✳ Instances of "state-confusion" can be traced back over centuries. *Incubus attacks are one example. The incubus would sit on the sleeper's chest, paralyze them, and then have sexual intercourse with them while they were asleep. In one medieval account, all the nuns at a convent reported being visited by an incubus.* Such experiences can feel very real and vivid but other more conventional explanations are now available.

SLEEP PARALYSIS

Contemporary research now recognizes that some paranormal sleep experiences are actually a physiological state called sleep paralysis. A normal aspect of REM sleep is that the body is immobilized, so that the person cannot act out their dreams. During sleep paralysis the body remains paralyzed, and the brain is still producing dreamlike images. People see, hear, and feel things, but cannot move, and feel that they are fully awake. A feeling of terror is often reported during the experience. The paralysis usually passes within a few minutes or even seconds.

you don't say

I was just powerless to move

DREAM INTERPRETATION: OBJECTIVE OR SUBJECTIVE?

✱ Even though dreams are one of the most reliably occurring forms of human consciousness, the links between dreams and parapsychology have caused some psychologists and scientists to undervalue them. The scientific community relies heavily on objectivity. Because it is impossible for researchers to get inside another person's dreams and observe them directly, this makes them difficult to study. However, there is now a growing number of researchers, especially in the U.S., who are systematically investigating dreams and helping us to understand how and why they are produced.

SCIENTIFIC METHOD

✱ The objectivity debate has also prevented dream interpretation from being taken seriously. *The process of interpreting a dream is very subjective, and what may*

scientists would like to get inside the dreams of other people to study them

"It is a curious irony in the history of psychology... that psychologists concerned with scientific evidence should conclude on the basis of folklore, as well as Freud's ostensibly unscientific analysis, that dream data were not a suitable phenomenon for scientific research."
ROBERT HASKELL (1951)

really!

dreams are as
unique as dreamers

have meaning for one person may have
no meaning for another.

✱ Another factor is that the process of
dream interpretation rests on one crucial
assumption—that dreams have personal

hmmm

it's impossible to
really get inside
someone's head

OBJECTIVE OR SUBJECTIVE

Objective reality is
seen as that which is
real and physical—
objects that exists
outside of the mind.
Subjective reality, in
contrast, is private and
personal. It includes
mental or cognitive
activity and feelings.
But are these things
any less real than solid
objects? Are there
ways of studying them
objectively?

meaning. Not all scientists accept this.
Crick and Mitchison (see page 46), suggest
that dream content is EPIPHENOMENA, a
series of random images. We can attach a
story to those images, but really they are
simply a consequence of the biological
process we call REM sleep. *However, some
cognitive psychologists regard dreaming as
the most reliably occurring form of human
consciousness and suggest that dreams can
teach us a lot about how the mind works.*

I just
don't know

I don't accept all
the current theories

69

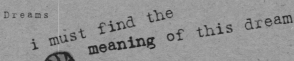

i must find the meaning of this dream

SEEING MEANING IN DREAMS

* Most people would instinctively disagree with the idea that dreams have no meaning. It is difficult to see dreams as meaningless because most of us have dreams that seem to relate directly to our lives.

INTERPRETATION METHODS

* In the 100 years since Freud developed his theory, the number of methods for interpreting dreams has grown significantly. *Some of these methods have proved so useful they have been employed in clinical settings to help people who are suffering from various forms of mental distress.*

* Why do we feel it is important to interpret dreams? The simple answer is that dreams seem to reveal something about us as individuals—about our lives, our relationships, about our past, or about current concerns that may be preoccupying us in our waking lives.

* *It has also been suggested that dreams reveal our deepest secrets—secrets that are hidden from us when we are awake but are made clear to us through our unconscious mind, which allows them to surface in the content of our dreams.*

it was so dreamy

"Dreams that are not interpreted are like letters which have not been opened. Dreams are important communications to ourselves."

Erich Fromm (1951)

DREAMS AS A WINDOW INTO OUR MIND

* This idea stems from the fact that dreams are our own creations. They are made when our brain is isolated from the waking world. During sleep, our brains create a world of their own, with its own characters, events, feelings, and outcomes: a world where anything can happen and often does.

* *Jung likened the world of dreams to each of us having our own theater where every night images unfold like a play, complete with stage, actors, and plot. And like any other play or story, dreams wait to be understood and interpreted.*

dreams are our own creation, the art of our sleeping hours

What's it all about?

There are probably as many theories or techniques about how to interpret dream content as there have been people to write them. They range from dream dictionary interpretations, where symbols are taken from the dream and used to imply general meanings, to the type of interpretation that can be achieved only when the dreamer is present and responds to various questions or probes in the presence of an analyst. Thus the dream is unraveled and given meaning.

I want to know your secrets

dreams can reveal our deepest secrets

THE SIGNIFICANCE OF DREAMS

* What kind of significance can we attach to dreams? There are many theories. Freud thought dreams were all about the negative aspects of human nature. For Carl Jung, dreams could lead to spiritual development and compensate for what was lacking in waking personality.

who was it?   um

every detail of a dream might be important

METAPHORS AND DREAMS

A metaphor is a theme, image, or symbol that stands for something else. For example, famous people may become metaphors for images associated with them. It has recently been reported that dreams in which Diana Princess of Wales appears often stand for motherhood, charity, and persecution. Other things to look for in dreams are sayings and analogies.

VARYING OPINIONS

* On the other hand, **Fritz Perls** wrote that every aspect of a dream could actually tell us something about dreamer's personality. **Calvin Hall** states that dreams are continuous with waking life and reflect the dreamer's current concerns, thoughts,

did you know that every aspect of your dream could tell us something about you?

and behaviors; a dream isn't ever an objective view of reality but it shows how the dreamer views the world. **Rosalind Cartwright** suggests that dreams serve an ADAPTIVE role, since they allow people to process emotionally significant information that relates to various life situations. A more eclectic approach is given by **Jeremy Taylor**, who says that there are at least 25 different ways that dreams can inform us about ourselves…

the objects that feature in our dreams can give clues

some symbols have a global significance

★ *Are there general meanings that apply to all dreams or do dreams only have individual significance?* There is no doubt that some symbols have general cultural meaning. Take, for example, a crucifix. This is a symbol of Christian faith, and would be recognized by most people as such. *So if someone has a dream about crucifixes, it would be reasonable to assume that the dream has some spiritual significance for them.*

Exploring dreams

The dictionary approach to dream interpretation only gives a very general idea as to what the dream is about. To make the interpretation more personal, it would be necessary to ask the dreamer what they were doing in the dream, who else was there, how they felt, what other objects there were, and what all this meant to the dreamer. After the dream has been thoroughly explored in this way, a very different meaning will emerge, one directly applicable to their own lives and relationships.

I must explore this dream in detail

THE FREUDIAN APPROACH

* Freud believed that dreams reflected desires and wishes that were unacceptable to the conscious waking mind, so that they appeared, disguised by the unconscious mind, in dreams. He felt that exploring them gave valuable insight into the dreamer's problems.

sex problems

day residue

Freud thought it was all about sex

FORGET IT

* One of the lesser known consequences of Freud's theory is that dreams are not really meant to be remembered at all. *The secret wishes are so potentially damaging to the dreamer that they are disguised in* the symbols that make up dreams. The satisfaction of these unfulfilled wishes is supposed to occur during sleep, out of consciousness, while the person is dreaming. But if a dream is recalled, then it can be worked with in psychoanalysis, and its hidden meaning accessed through DREAM WORK.

this psychological distress is so distressing

a dream is a symptom of psychological distress, according to Freud

FREUD'S LEGACY

★ Freud thought that dream content represented NEUROSIS, and that dreams, once they had been interpreted, showed the source of psychological distress. *In other words, the dream is a symptom of a psychological problem.* The dream usually represents an unfulfilled wish.

★ It was this idea that made dreams a valuable clinical tool. And while dream interpretation has changed significantly since Freud's era, his work is still influential in the field. The whole idea that dreams represent the unconscious mind, and that they can be used in therapy, really is a Freudian legacy. *Most people these days do not value Freud's work highly, but he should be recognized for his valuable contribution to our understanding of how dreams work.*

I wish I could remember

LATENT AND MANIFEST

Freud differentiated between the latent and manifest content of dreams. The manifest meaning of a dream would probably relate to what he called "day residue." The latent dream allowed the dreamer to discharge repressed energy (usually sexual energy).

75

JUNG: ACCENTUATING THE POSITIVE

★ Jung's theory of dream interpretation has become increasingly popular since the late 1970s. However, it is complicated and sometimes difficult to grasp. This is a much more positive approach to dream meaning; Jung believed that dreams were the normal expression of emotionally relevant information.

Carl Jung

PROSPECTIVE POWER

Jung also said that dreams have a prospective power. This doesn't mean that they have a mysterious ability to foretell the future (although some people do use this part of the theory in this way); it means they have the power to show possibilities. Hence dreams are also visions of future potential.

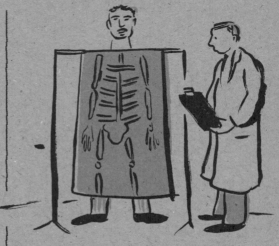

the dream shows the dreamer's inner state

JUNG'S VIEW OF DREAMS

★ Jung's ideas differ from Freud's in several key respects. For example, he believed that the manifest dream was an honest representation of the dreamer's inner state. *The reason that the content of dreams can be so confusing is because dreams use the language of the unconscious, which can seem illogical to*

Jung said that dreams help to balance the conscious and unconscious mind

Topographical theories

Both Freud's and Jung's theories are topographical because they try to portray the mind as a territory or map. They identify allotted areas that perform specific functions. Freud's theory describes unconsciousness, consciousness, and preconsciousness and the parts of the personality that reside in them: the Id, the Ego, and the Superego. Jung described two general types of consciousness. First, there is a personal or individual consciousness, comprising both conscious and unconscious realms. Second, there is a collective unconscious that each of us can tap into. This was the deepest layer of the psyche.

us when we try to understand the dream in our conscious state. The language of the unconscious is symbolic, and the goal of dream interpretation is to translate the symbolic meaning of the dream so that its meaning becomes clear.

BALANCING ACT

✱ Jung stated that the most important function of dreams was to compensate. *Imbalances exist between the conscious and unconscious mind. But for a person to be psychologically healthy the mind must reach a state of equilibrium.* Dreams serve as a powerful tool in this balancing process. This is because dreams can bring into awareness emotions or issues to which the dreamer has not paid enough attention in his or her waking life.

this map must be wrong

ARCHETYPES

* The aspect of Jung's theory that is perhaps most well known is his ideas about archetypes. These are primordial images that have been found throughout history and across cultures. They are universal thought forms and feelings that link humanity together.

hero

the hero

Mythic figures

There are many other archetypes that present themselves during dreams, including the Great Mother, the Father, the Wise Old Man, the Hero, God, the Trickster, Rebirth and Reincarnation, along with many others. Understanding the nature of archetypes is helped by myths, religions, and dreams.

PRIMORDIAL IMAGES

* Archetypes are present at birth, stored in the UNCONSCIOUS REALM. They appear as symbols in dreams and show concerns that have been present for humans since the evolution of the species. Some common archetypes are:

The Persona: This is often present as the social aspect of ourselves. Also known as the mask—the face (or faces) that we show to the world. A good example of the persona is an image of a smiling face that quickly reverses to show a sad face. Another representation of the persona is the clown.

The Shadow: This is often represented as the dark side of the self, the parts of us that we find hard to acknowledge.

The Anima and Animus: Both men and women have qualities that are associated with their sex. For example, men are often seen as aggressive, powerful, and strong, and women as gentle, caring, and emotional.

the persona   the shadow   the animus   the self   mandalas

Jung's archetypes reside in the collective unconscious

BIG DREAMS AND LITTLE DREAMS

Jung said that people had "big" and "little" dreams. A "little" dream relates to the "personal." It usually contains people, places, and feelings that relate to waking life. Little dreams are often forgotten quickly. They can, however, perform the functions of compensation or of showing us future possibilities. Big dreams, on the other hand, relate to the collective unconscious. These are usually archetypal dreams. They help us in the process of individuation. Big dreams are those that we recall over a lifetime.

Jung believed that each sex carried the biological and psychological elements of the other. The anima is the representation of the female in men. The animus is the representation of men in women.

The Self: The center of personality. This includes both conscious and unconscious, and attracts the other archetypes, elements of the personality (i.e., good and bad, old and young, introvert and extrovert). What we experience as "I," or "Me."

Mandalas: A mandala is a "magic circle." It stands for the unity of the Self. As we are all individuals we will each have a different mandala. The symmetry of the mandala stands for perfection of the self; the goal we all strive toward.

it was only a little dream

79

JUNGIAN AMPLIFICATION

* Freud used the technique of free association, looking for loose connections with the content of the dream. Jung was more specific, using the process of amplification. Instead of looking for hidden meanings in the dream content, Jung asked the dreamer to describe the personal meaning of the symbol or image, and then link this to the waking world. He also looked for collective content and how this might lead to archetypal meaning. He called this personal and collective amplification.

MEDITATION

* Jung might also suggest meditating on the symbols in the dream, or opening an internal dialogue with them. His most salient point is that *only the dreamer knows what the dream means* and how it should be interpreted. The outcome of any interpretation should be to add something to the dreamer's life.

only you know
the meaning of your dreams

"To me, dreams are a part of nature which harbor no intention to deceive, but express something as best they can, just as a plant grows or as an animal seeks food as best it can."

Carl Jung (1965)

a dream about black and white dogs could be amplified in many ways

DIFFERENCES BETWEEN FREUD AND JUNG

✱ *There are various differences between the ideas of Freud and Jung.*

✱ Freud believed that the meaning of the dream was hidden. *Jung argued that the manifest dream showed the actual state of the dreamer's inner world.*

✱ Freud believed that dreams showed the negative aspects of human nature, because they were a symptom of neurosis. *Jung argued that dreams serve the process of individuation, by compensating for aspects of the self that were in need of balance. Hence they help in the integration of the various aspects of the psyche.*

✱ Freud used the technique of free association in interpretation. *However, Jung believed free association took the dreamer away from the dream's true meaning. Instead, Jung used amplification, which intensified the meaning of each dream symbol.*

PERSONAL AND COLLECTIVE AMPLIFICATION

The dream: I dreamed of a black and white dog.

Personal amplification: I had a small dog when I was child, which I really loved. It reminds me of feeling safe and of going on long walks with my family. It reminds me...

Collective amplification: A black and white dog represents opposites of good and evil, day and night, ying and yang, death and life. The dog could be interpreted in myths, such as the story of the good shepherd and his dog, who protect the flock. There are many other stories that this could link to, but this gives a general example of how amplification might work.

yin-yang is the Chinese theory of life harmony

FRITZ PERLS

✱ Fritz Perls was the charismatic founder of Gestalt therapy. He was epecially known for his exuberant and imaginative style of working with people in therapy. Gestalt therapy focuses on "the whole" and integrating "the sum of its parts." His ideas about dreams were very definite (as were his ideas about most things!). He states that no part of a dream is meaningless, and that everything appears for the purpose of integrating the whole personality.

> "The dream is an existential message ... of yourself, to yourself."
>
> Fritz Perls, 1970

EMPTY CHAIR TECHNIQUE

Two chairs are placed facing each other. The dreamer first sits in one and talks to a person or object that they described in the dream, saying what they want to. Then they move to the other chair and respond as they think that person or object would. This continues until the situation is resolved.

the empty chair technique

GESTALT THERAPY

✱ The Gestalt (the German word for *figure* or *form*) techniques that Perls developed are very useful when it comes to dream interpretation. The method assumes that every element of the dream is a projected part of the dreamer's personality. *Thus with understanding and exploration it may be possible to integrate them back into the "Gestalt."*

Gestalt therapy is about
putting the pieces back
together to restore the form

* There are a number of different techniques used in Gestalt therapy:

1 Asking the dreamer to tell the dream using the first person and present tense. For example "I am walking in a wood, it is morning…"

2 Getting the dreamer to role-play objects in the dream. For example, saying what it feels like to be a tree in the wood.

3 Asking the dreamer for detailed descriptions of thoughts, feelings, actions, and duty felt toward each object in the dream.

4 Involving the dreamer in dialogues with "split-off" elements of the self in the dream, so that they can be reintegrated and benefit the whole personality.

5 The dreamer identifies opposites in the dream, which may indicate where conflict lies.

TOP DOG

Another technique that is often used in dream interpretation using Gestalt techniques is to identify the top dog and the underdog. The top dog is the part of the personality that thinks it is superior. It is often the judge, and critical of the decisions made by the dreamer. The underdog on the other hand is the oppressed part of the person. It can often be represented as a child, or someone who is striving to "do better next time." If this were identified in dream content, it could be useful to use the "empty chair" technique to get a dialogue going and see what insight this might bring.

I am the superior dog

83

ANN FARADAY: THE THREE FACES OF DREAMING

* Ann Faraday is truly a pioneer in dream interpretation. In the 1970s she wrote two books, *Dream Power* and *The Dream Game*, which continue to change attitudes toward dreams and dream work.

Faraday says there are three aspects of dreaming

EXISTENTIAL MESSAGES

Existential life issues are the "facts of life" that everyone has to face at some time or other.
1 Everything is impermanent.
2 We are all ultimately alone.
3 All life is meaningless.
4 We must all face death.
Existentialists believe that at some point during life these issues must be faced. Their presence is heralded by angst, or emotional discomfort. Failure to look at them can result in psychological or emotional dysfunction.

TRIPARTITE SYSTEM

* Faraday believes that dreams have three layers of meaning, each of which should be explored. It is important to interpret all three potential meanings of the dream.

* Level 1: Looking outward
Looking outward from the dream involves looking to see whether the dream tells us anything about the objective world of the dreamer. Dreams often depict external events that were not addressed during waking. The meanings of dreams are often direct, and looking outward from a dream often acts as a reminder or warning, and may show the true nature of people. *Faraday also states that dreams can be clairvoyant and precognitive, incorporating aspects that she liked of Jung's prospective function of dreams.*

✳ Level 2: Looking-glass dreams

This aspect of the method is taken from the book *Alice through the Looking Glass*, and refers to the unique perception of the world that each of us has. Primarily, this level of the dream shows the dreamer who they truly are. *The interpretation of the "looking-glass self" is often best achieved through elements like dream characters, dream animals, houses or settings, modes of transportation, and how the dreamer appears.* Each of these elements can be used to show the individual's relationship, both good and bad, with the world.

✳ Level 3: Looking inward

In many ways levels 1 and 2 deal with what is. Level 3 deals with the conflicts in our personality, and our potential for changing or resolving them. *Faraday makes no secret of her reliance on Gestalt techniques for uncovering this aspect of dreams. This involves opening dialogues with dream characters, and identifying "top dog vs. underdog" scenarios. These may emerge and provide the real key to interpretation if the dream images or symbols are allowed to speak for themselves.* Conflicts or opposites are sought and explored. These methods will often allow the dream's EXISTENTIAL MESSAGE to unfold.

what a view

the 2nd level of meaning is about our view of the world

Buried treasure

The final stage is to uncover the dream's "buried treasure," and thus allow the dream to help us integrate what it represents back into the whole. This level of dream work can be very useful to help understand nightmares or recurring dreams.

we should uncover the buried treasure of our dream

GAYLE DELANEY:
THE DREAM INTERVIEW

✳ Gayle Delaney is one of the founders of the
Delaney and Flowers Dream Center in San Francisco.
She has written several books including *In Your
Dreams* and *Sexual dreams*. She is also a founding
member and past president of the Association for the
Study of Dreams. She believes that dreams are
personalized views of salient issues in the dreamer's
life. Her method is simple and easy to learn, using
several well-defined steps, which all come together
to form what she calls the "the dream interview."

I see a link

SETTING OUT THE DREAM DIAGRAM

✳ The process begins by DREAM DIAGRAMMING. This involves writing down the dream and highlighting key components of it using various codes. *She suggests underlining the setting(s), circling the main characters, highlighting major objects, drawing wavy lines underneath feelings and emotions, and indicating with an arrow the major actions in the dream.* An example is given here.

✳ After this the actual INTERVIEW begins. The dreamer starts by retelling the dream in the first person

I was walking with my mother and father in
our old house. We were in the kitchen. In
the center of the room was a large table, with
four seats around it. Mom and Dad were
talking and I was looking for something in
the cupboards above my head. I felt like I
had lost something but was comforted by
the presence of my parents.

alien

and present tense. This helps to restimulate the memory of the dream and actively involves the dreamer in the dream. This is then followed by 6 more questions:

1 **What are the feelings in the dream?**
2 **What are the settings in the dream like?**
3 **Who are the people in the dream?**
4 **What objects does the dream contain?**
5 **What events are taking place?**

you should describe your dream as if you were talking to an alien

✳ *At each point in this part of the process, after the description of each of the elements listed, the dreamer is asked if he can see any links between the dream and situations or relationships in his own life.*

✳ After there has been a thorough investigation of the dream, the listener then retells the dream to the dreamer, as she understands it from what she has been told. As far as possible she should try to use the same language as the dreamer. ***This should result in an "A-ha" experience. In other words the interpretation should cause the dreamer to feel enlightened in some way by the dream's message or content.*** Finally, the dreamer is asked:

6 **What do you understand this dream to mean?**

TELLING THE DREAM

The description of the dream should include details of the setting, people, objects, feelings, and actions. One of Delaney's directives is that the description should be delivered as if to an alien from another planet, someone who has never had any dealings with any of the elements that the dreamer is describing. This should ensure that no essential details are missed.

MONTAGUE ULLMAN: COMMUNITY DREAM WORK

✻ So far we have talked about dreams mainly in reference to the individual. One of the main tenets of Montague Ullman's work is that dreams, and dream sharing, are inherently social activities. Thus dream work in groups can raise social and political consciousness. By directly looking at the links between dreams and racism and sexism, just about any "ism" can be addressed. Ullman states that dreams help a person to adapt to their social position.

TWO HEADS ARE BETTER THAN ONE

how enlightening

yes I see

☆ WOW

✻ Ullman's recipe for a dream group has been adopted by the Association for the Study of Dreams and is available to anyone who wishes to begin a dream group in his area. This method is great fun and is suitable for children, teenagers, and adults. Ullman believes that dreams are a way of resolving emotional problems. *Like Jung he believes that dreams communicate metaphorically, and as such they can have many meanings. The job of the dream group is to unravel the possibilities and help the dreamer to reach some understanding of the dream.*

group dream work allows for a range of interpretations

✱ After a dream has been described, the other members of the group make associations of their own, *as if it had been their dream*. They talk about the feelings **they** got from the dream, without ever saying "I think your dream means...." The original dreamer can then take what she wants from the group, in terms of interpretations that fit for her. There is no need for a dream expert, although it probably helps if someone is there who has experience of working with dreams.

group work can help dreamers to work out their own dreams

WORKING WITH DREAMS TODAY

✱ These brief descriptions of the methods used by Faraday, Delaney, and Ullman give a flavor of the possibilities that are available. There are several points upon which most writers agree. *First, modern dream interpreters include and build upon the techniques of their predecessors. Second, all the writers agree that dreams can help the individual in the process of self-development.*

modern dream workers build on what has gone before

Dreams are personal

Finally, every dream should really be interpreted in terms of the dreamer's life. There are no such things as universal meanings for dream images and symbols. Ideally, a dream should be interpreted with the dreamer present. In the absence of this, any understanding is a generalization, and may not apply to the dreamer's life.

89

THE USE OF DREAMS IN A CLINICAL SETTING

✱ If people are upset, depressed, traumatized, or under some kind of psychological or physical stress, one of the first things that will be affected is the quality of their sleep. Alongside changes in sleep pattern, people often report changes in dream-recall rate, increased intensity of dream feelings, and changes in dream vividness. These changes in sleep and dream life may be among the first indicators that "something is wrong," and may lead to a visit to the doctor, or into some form of therapy.

disaster area

distressing events can trigger repeated terrifying dreams

TRAUMATIC DREAMS

The traumatic dream was the one exception that Freud made in his theory about dreams as wish fulfillment. He said the meaning of such dreams was literal.

TRAUMATIC DREAMS

✱ In extreme cases—for instance, trauma or drug withdrawal—these changes can be sudden and distressing. *It is often the case after a traumatic incident that the event is replayed over and over again during the person's dreams. This is especially true if the event was life threatening, and other people were killed.* Such dreams are often experienced as exact replications of the event, and are sometimes replayed several times each night. This type of dream can be one of the first indicators of post-traumatic stress disorder.

RECOVERY

* A dream worker called Barry Krakow has developed a pioneering technique called IMAGERY REHEARSAL TREATMENT, which he uses with men and women who have suffered terrible nightmares as a result of traumatic life events. *In the waking state dreamers recall in detail their recurring nightmares, and change the imagery so that it becomes more positive and less distressing. In a group setting they create a new dream, which they rehearse several times a day until the new daydream takes the place of the old nightmare.* This technique has been very helpful in reducing post-traumatic nightmares.

* *However, if the view is taken that all dreams come in the service of psychological health, the power of these dreams begins to emerge when people start to use them to understand apparently negative situations in their lives.* If they start talking about them with others in a similar situation, they may be able to identify

recurring nightmares can make people afraid to sleep

problems and solutions. Ullman's group method is ideal for this. The dreamers can start to develop strategies. *Negative dreams are now put to good use and utilized in the process of self development.*

alcohol can cause sleep problems

Drugs and drink

Alcohol interferes with the natural sleep cycle. It makes people sleep more heavily during the first part of the night, and increases the intensity of REM sleep during the second part, making people wake up, and remember their dreams. People who have stopped drinking after being heavy drinkers suffer a rebound effect, that makes it difficult to sleep and leads to very frightening dreams. Withdrawal from drugs produces the same effect, and women can have particularly emotionally unpleasant dreams during drug withdrawal. Research has shown that withdrawal dreams are full of self-hate and aggression, and often include drinking. People sometimes wake up not sure if they have drunk or not. The boundary between waking and sleeping reality has become blurred.

91

men have aggressive
dreams

TYPICAL?

You may think that some of these sex differences in dream content are stereotypical. This is one of the criticisms that have been made against Hall and Van de Castle's work. Another is that their method doesn't describe the emotional content of the dreams very well. However, this is a classic dream study that has been used and replicated in many countries. One of its strengths is that it allows us to describe the typical content of a large number of dreams.

WHAT DO PEOPLE DREAM ABOUT?

* In contrast to the dreams of people in great distress-trauma dreams, for instance, or dreams during drug withdrawal-what do "typical" people dream about, every day? To answer this we need to look at the content of large numbers of dreams.

GENDER ROLES

* A classic study in dream interpretation was conducted by Calvin Hall and Robert Van de Castle in 1966. They analyzed the content of 5 dreams each from 100 male and 100 female American students, and documented their most common dream content. They found that men and women reported dreaming about different things.

I dreamed of home

women's dreams usually have
a domestic setting

men's dreams are often set outdoors

✱ According to this study, the settings for men's dreams are often places they know that are outdoors. On average, men's dreams tend to contain more male than female characters. Interactions with dream characters are often physically aggressive. *Men report more rejection in their dreams than women, and more sexual activity.*

✱ Contrary to men's dreams, women's dreams are set indoors, but like men's, the settings are familiar. **Women's dreams differ in several significant ways from those of men.** Women's dreams contain similar numbers of male and female characters. But women more often dream of people they know. Women's dreams are less aggressive and more friendly than men's, especially in terms of "helping and protecting" other dream characters.

woman dream about nurturing

The same dreams

Hall and Van de Castle have used this method of content analysis to interpret long series of dreams from one person. They studied one woman's dreams, over her life, from the age of 25 until she was 78. Over this time, "Dorothea" reported 904 dreams. Using the content analysis method, they found that dream content not only is continuous with waking life but is consistent. In other words, we dream about the same things over and over again.

93

aughhhh!

fear is the commonest
feeling in dreams

dreams can be about
"nice" everyday things

CHAPTER 6
DREAM THEMES

* While the detailed content
of dreams may tell us one story
about our dreams, another useful
way of trying to understand
what dreams mean is to look
at their themes.

UNIVERSAL DREAM THEMES

* By far the most common theme people
report is being in danger. They may be
hurt, dying, or dead in a dream. Other
general themes are being chased, being in

water is a very common
dream setting

water or surrounded by it, being lost, flying
through the air, eating, finding money,
being naked in public, and having one's
teeth fall out. *These types of dreams tend
to be somewhat unpleasant.* Nicer dreams
involve family outings, going to public
functions, being with famous people, and
of course dreaming of having sex.

WOW!

finding money is an obvious
wish-fulfillment dream

✱ Because these dream stories have occurred over and over again throughout history, they are often the dreams that dream researchers are asked to interpret. *Hence, since the beginning of dream interpretation, dozens of leading dream analysts have offered their opinions on what particular themes represent.*

✱ In the rest of this book we will look at 23 of the most common themes and explore what different dream researchers have had to say about their possible meanings.

I think I'm lost

exam in progress →

sorry I'm late...

THEME 1: TAKING AN EXAM

* "I remember arriving at a high school I used to attend. I had to take an exam that I had only just found out about. I didn't feel prepared at all. I kept getting lost but eventually found the right room. There were two examiners, a man and a woman, they both looked very forbidding. I felt really anxious, and worried. I just knew I wasn't ready for what lay ahead of me. I also knew that the teachers would be really angry if I failed."

it's so humiliating

BE PREPARED

* Exam dreams are very common. The student doesn't feel prepared for what is about to happen, causing them to feel anxious. Sometimes they don't realize until the very last minute that they don't have the information they need. Occasionally they may even have prepared for the exam, well in advance, only to find that they have studied the wrong subject, or can't remember what they have learned.

Dreams of the same type, with similar meaning, are going out onto a stage and forgetting the words, or finding oneself unprepared for some public task, such as giving a speech.

✱ Using the case study above, a Freudian interpretation of such a dream would be that the examiners were the dreamer's mother and father (or other authority figures), and the sense of failure was about not meeting parental expectations. *If the exam was about biology or anatomy, then the dream is linked to unconscious sexual guilt. The humiliation felt at not being able to complete the exam represents the fulfillment of a wish for the dreamer, who wants to be punished for some type of sexual misconduct.* The idea of an "examiner," and having the "right answers," are also very reminiscent of the Superego assessing conduct and delivering its verdict.

a dream examiner might represent your parents

Wish fulfillment

Freud actually wrote about a lawyer with whom he had been to college, who came to one of his lectures. At school Freud had always achieved higher grades than this man. After the lecture the lawyer dreamed of losing every case he defended. The lawyer argued that if Freud's wish-fulfillment theory was correct then he should have dreams in which he won all his cases, thus fulfilling his desires to win. Freud responded by saying that, on the contrary, this dream supported his theory because the dreamer really had a desire to humiliate Freud and prove him wrong. And Freud said that this dream did just that. It fulfilled his wish for Freud to be wrong, and allowed the lawyer to be better than Freud for once.

embarrassing biology exams might be a sign of sexual guilt

97

wow, look
at her

Freud suggests that
exam dreams are
associated with
teenage sexuality

TOP MARKS

Calvin Hall and
William Domhoff
propose that dreams
reflect waking life.
People who have such
dreams are those who
are facing a test of
some kind. On the
bright side for those
who are actually facing
exams, research has
shown that students
who experience exam
dreams tend to get
better marks!

PASSING THE TEST

✻ Most people associate exams with
finishing high school or college at the end
of their adolescence. This is the stage
between childhood and maturity, the
time when young people begin to
explore their sexuality and
masturbation begins. Freud suggested
that guilt from sexual misconduct,
namely masturbation, is what exam
dreams are all about. *If the dreamer is
male and holding a pen, the symbolism
becomes obvious. In this case, the dream
is a symptom of sexual guilt.*

✻ A less Freudian interpretation, but
one that still focuses on adolescence and
the transition from one life stage to
another, is the idea of having all the
necessary knowledge for the "TEST OF LIFE"
but not actually feeling ready to move
forward into adulthood and all its
responsibilities. This may be true for many
people who are facing a life transition, not
just teenagers.

come on, answer
the question

facing a challenging aspect of life
might produce exam stress dreams

✱ Jungian psychology offers a more optimistic interpretation. Exams are really about "the examiner within." This may relate to the HIGHER SELF or even God, the part of ourselves that knows the right answer. Because the exam setting is all about performing under pressure, it may ask if the dreamer can answer a question as yet unseen. Exam dreams can often relate to whether we would do the right thing at the right time.

I should know this...

not knowing the answer might be symbolic of a more general feeling of uncertainty

the exam dream might be about an opportunity to succeed in waking life

✱ *Gayle Delaney suggests that we should ask the dreamer if he or she is in fact going to take an examination in the near future. It may be that the person lacks confidence about this test, or has a tendency toward perfectionism.*

EXAM BLUES

During exam dreams there is something very unsettling about not having an answer that one is expected to know. For many, this leads to a classic anxiety rush, and the thought "I should know this!" The dream may be a metaphor for feeling out of one's depth, in a situation where the dreamer feels he should have the ability to succeed, or at least be prepared.

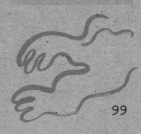

THEME 2: PUBLIC NAKEDNESS

* "I am standing naked in an empty room. I see a closed door in front of me. I walk through it and find myself in the middle of a busy street. I am mortified that I am naked, and I have no way of covering myself up. There are people everywhere, but no one seems to notice me, even though I feel much bigger than I actually am, and there is nowhere to hide."

MEN HAVE MORE

Studies show that men have more naked dreams than women. If we look at the interpretations here, we could say that this is a gender difference that results from men's fear of being vulnerable. This may metaphorically translate itself into their experiencing more nakedness in their dreams.

standing out from the crowd

different cultures have different ideas about nudity

COVERING UP

* The common elements of such dreams are that the person is naked, usually in front of people he doesn't know. The other dream characters appear unmoved by the nudity and may even ignore it. The dreamer usually feels embarrassed and anxious as he tries to cover up. Occasionally, the dreamer reports feeling proud of his body and confident if onlookers stare at them.

✱ Nakedness has different meanings in different cultures; to understand its significance in a dream, we should try to understand the meaning of being clothed or covered up. *We are all born naked, and only learn to feel embarrassed by our exposed bodies as we take on the values and norms of our society. In our culture nudity is forbidden, even illegal in some situations. But it is also acceptable in the "right place," usually a sexual situation. In this context the perfectly proportioned, unclothed body is highly valued, even aspired to, as it encourages sexual desire.*

dream nakedness might mean a desire for a more natural lifestyle

A TYPICAL DREAM

✱ Freud described naked dreams as "typical." He felt they were probably stimulated by an actual memory of when the dreamer was caught naked by his parents during childhood—or by the early memory of a medical examination by a physician for some childhood ailment, when the child felt exposed. Freud said that all children have EXHIBITIONIST TENDENCIES, when they feel free of conflict or shame about their bodies. So nakedness in dreams indicates a wish to return to a more carefree and irresponsible period in our lives.

See me naked...

A more psychological interpretation given by Freud was that dreamers had a wish to be seen naked by those they were attracted to. But they protect themselves from this wish by appearing naked in front of complete strangers. He called this a "contrary wish." The disguised objects of affection are much less threatening to the ego, and allow the dreamers to deal with the wish as satisfactorily as possible.

clothes are a
form of self-
protection

THE MEANING OF CLOTHES

Nakedness is covered with clothing, a symbol that itself can have a whole range of meanings. For example, uniforms, formal evening wear, and casual clothes all have different connotations, and their own socially acceptable uses. So losing our clothes may indicate that we have left our various social roles behind and appear as we were at birth, exposed, with none of the fronts we usually hide behind.

RING OF CONFIDENCE

✱ Gayle Delaney doesn't support Freud's interpretation. She suggests that these dreams rarely involve a wish for nudity. They actually represent anxiety and show that the dreamer feels vulnerable in front of others. *She interprets the indifferent reaction of the onlookers as an indication that the dreamer feels his concerns about how others may react to his exposure to be unwarranted or exaggerated.* In terms of nudity and feelings of confidence, Delaney says that this can show that the person is comfortable with his body, and may even indicate confidence in his sexuality. There is something very liberating about standing in front of

there's little point in exposing yourself

others, completely exposed, but still feeling confident.

* *Alfred Adler suggests that the key to naked dreams is that they allow our most personal imperfections to be seen. They show a fear of intimacy, and of being seen without all the trappings (psychological and material) that we use to cover up our imperfections.*

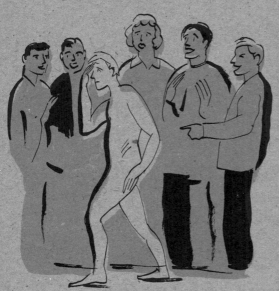

the reaction of onlookers in the dream suggests what the dreamer feels about themselves

This is me

One of the most pragmatic explanations of nakedness in dreams comes from Robert Van de Castle. He says that clothing in dreams represents identity. In this case, clothing makes a statement about who we are, and nakedness in a dream should be seen as asking: "What would people think of me if they could see me as I really am underneath?" He also allows a more individual interpretation of the dream as indicated by the reaction of other dream characters to the nudity. So, if the dreamer is surrounded by strangers and ignored, it may mean that there is little point in exposing one's deepest self to acquaintances. If the dreamer is ridiculed for being naked and the dreamer knows the observers, it might be a warning of insincerity in those people. Finally, if the dreamer feels confident, it means that their assurance supports him even when there is nothing to hide behind.

103

THEME 3: CHANGING SEX

ARGGHH!

* "I am getting undressed. I look at my body and notice that my breasts are getting smaller, and to my horror I have a penis! I realize that I am changing sex. My feminine attributes are disappearing and I am becoming a man."

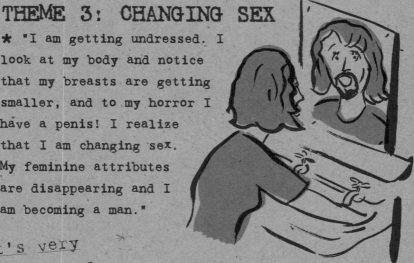

it's very bizarre...

sex-change dreams may be about male and female aspects of our personality

sex-change dreams are very unsettling

A HECK OF A SHOCK

* The common feature of dreams where the dreamer, or another character, changes sex, or has the attributes of the opposite sex, is the intense feeling of BIZARRENESS that accompanies them. The dreamer often awakens feeling strange and a bit disorientated, and ponders on how strange the dream was.

* In the dream the person is getting undressed, and realizes that she has physical aspects of the opposite sex. She is shocked by this, and displeased. The first person we can look to for an interpretation of this dream is Carl Jung. A Jungian interpretation may be as follows: as the PERSONA is dropped (i.e., nakedness) the masculine aspects of personality develop (animus).

* It may be that the woman in our example is overly feminine. For her personality to be balanced she may need to drop this mask (persona), and develop some masculine attributes. This would result in a more whole being, with more resources at her disposal. *So the dream warns the female dreamer of an imbalance in her personality and compensates for this by changing the dreamer's physical attributes in the dream. This causes a strong emotional reaction, drawing attention to the imbalance and presenting an opportunity to explore it.*

gender dreams are about balance

SEX AND GENDER

"Sex" is used to refer to the physiological characteristics that we are born with. This is ascribed and cannot be changed. "Gender" refers to the way we learn to behave in relation to our sex (known as expected gender role). This may be different dependent upon where, or when, you are brought up.

for a woman to dream about becoming a man might suggest that she needs to explore her masculine side

i'm all woman

Oedipus

OVER TO FREUD

✱ A Freudian interpretation would lead to a possible fixation in the PHALLIC STAGE of development. The most probable interpretation would be that the dream shows clear penis envy on the part of the dreamer, who, in an attempt to disguise the wish for a penis, reacts in horror when she finds that she has one. The dreamer is stuck in an ELECTRA COMPLEX. Basically, this involves the girl's growing awareness as she develops that she doesn't have a penis. This causes her to feel inferior to men, and to identify with her mother who also shares her "defect."

if only...

Freud would claim that sex-change dreams indicate a woman's secret desire for a penis

what!?

some would argue
that sex-change
dreams result
from confusion
in the dreaming
brain

✱ *A cognitive interpretation of this dream would suggest a mismatch of images. This approach would argue that dreams are bizarre and have little meaning. The part of the brain that produces images has gotten confused, and this has resulted in the image.*

✱ Stanley Krippner has investigated the dream content of people with SEXUAL IDENTITY DISORDER (for example, people that want to change their sex) and found that their dream content reflects aspects of both sexes. *They share some fundamental similarities with their own sex but also dream about being their desired sexual identity.* He would also argue that dreams like these can be used to address dreamers' sexual stereotypes.

Gender agenda

Those who suggest that dreams link with waking thoughts and feelings may say that this dream relates to issues about the dreamer's gender identity. There may be some anxiety surrounding the person's femininity. In direct contrast to the Jungian compensation theory, perhaps the dreamer feels she is too masculine, or perhaps she has been accused of acting outside her expected gender role. This may cause her to incorporate her feelings about this into dream content.

✱ you are too **masculine**

107

THEME 4: LOSING TEETH

* "I am standing looking at myself in a mirror. I suddenly realize that some of the teeth in my mouth are crumbling, while others are falling out whole. I feel very distressed by this. I put my hand to my mouth but can't stop what is happening. I wonder how I will be able to smile ever again."

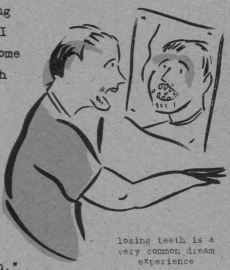

losing teeth is a very common dream experience

A COMMON DREAM

* This is probably one of the most common dreams, with most people having experienced it at one time or another. Dreams containing hair loss are often taken to have the same meaning. Interestingly, this is one of the dreams that has been mentioned throughout history, beginning with Artemidorus, who wrote

teeth are symbols of power and potency

Oneirocriteria (*The Interpretation of Dreams*) centuries ago. He said that dreams of the upper teeth were about householders, while lower teeth represented the slaves or workers. Loss of either set of teeth was an indication of upheaval in that part of the household; the loss of both sets might indicate loss of power for the house.

✻ In terms of Freudian theory the meaning of tooth loss (or the loss of any part of the body) is clear: It represents <u>CASTRATION</u>

Freud

<u>ANXIETY</u>. But Freudian theory is renowned for its lack of empirical support. Because of the inability to conduct studies to support psycho-analytic theory, it has been labeled "pseudo-science." *However, teeth dreams allow his theory of castration anxiety to be tested: Freud stated that women would have less castration anxiety than men, for obvious reasons.* It follows, then, that they will have fewer dreams where they lose their teeth, or other body parts.

✻ Calvin Hall tested this idea by looking at the dreams of hundreds of men and women, and counted the number of times they mentioned loss of parts of the body. *He found that men reported such losses three times more often than women, thus supporting Freud's castration-anxiety hypothesis.*

A Great Misfortune

For Hall, the overarching theme of "teeth dreams" is loss. He also points out that we should not be surprised by such dreams, since our teeth do fall out at various times in our lives. Using his content analysis method, the loss of teeth is coded as a misfortune. This is defined as an event that happens through no fault of the dreamer, or any other dream character. Hall believes that misfortunes in dreams can be an indication of wishing to be punished, but not wanting to blame oneself or anyone else. Thus tooth loss provides the appropriate situation for expressing masochistic tendencies.

OTHER IDEAS

✱ Sometimes showing or baring teeth is an aggressive gesture. **In China this is a symbol for warfare.** In other cultures teeth are extracted from the body just before burial. This is because teeth are the most enduring part of the body and their removal signifies the end of life. If we accept Perl's idea that each object in a dream is part of the dreamer, then loss of teeth may show the death of some enduring aspect of the dreamer's personality.

✱ *Some psychologists accept Calvin Hall's interpretation but are more specific about the nature of the loss. They suggest that*

baring the teeth is an aggressive
gesture, so losing them in a dream
might indicate loss of strength

HONORING THE DREAM

A lot of information presented about what dreams mean suggests that dreams are trying to bring into conscious awareness issues that are important in the dreamer's life. One of the way that this can be acknowledged is by "honoring the dream." To honor a dream you act upon its content. For example, if you have a dream that strongly focuses "red," you can buy yourself an item of red clothing and wear it. Or perhaps a particular image is salient; if so draw it— use the dream to develop artistic inclinations. Perhaps the dream shows you acting in a manner that is unusual for you. To honor the dream you carry this behavior into waking life (within sensible limits!). You consciously acknowledge the dream; the dream has fulfilled its purpose.

fear of aging might be behind
some tooth-loss dreams

dreams in which teeth fall out are
metaphors for loss of power.

✱ Kevin Todeshi distinguishes between
the types of teeth that are lost. If they are
baby teeth, then the dream may signify

just a few more
extractions...

a move from
childhood to
maturity. If they are
old teeth, it may
indicate a fear of old
age. False teeth can
mean false words, or
words that should
not be believed.

Fading powers

Alan Seigel agrees that
dreams of teeth are a
universal theme. Such
dreams can symbolize
physical or emotional
injury. They may also
mean a loss of power
and identity, a case of
"losing face." But he
tempers these negative
meanings by saying that
if the dreamer sees new
teeth hiding underneath
the old ones, or even
feels new teeth grow,
then this can mean the
loss of an old way of
being and the discovery
of stronger ability
underneath. Another
issue emerges: that
teeth are very important
for our appearance.
Loss of teeth may show
a fear of becoming
unattractive. This has
been discussed by some
writers in terms of a
fear of aging and loss
of the conventional
image of beauty.

THEME 5: FAMOUS PEOPLE IN DREAMS

* "I am at a party. I look across the room and I see several famous people gathered together. I first notice Monica from *Friends*. Then I see Marilyn Monroe. They are arguing. I see the Princess of Wales go up to them and try to join the group. Frank Sinatra is singing in the background but no one is listening to him. I felt really honored to be in the same place as all these people."

but I'm a great cook

WHAT A SWELL PARTY THIS IS

* One of the most striking features of this dream is the diversity of famous people in it. *Monica from* Friends *is a great cook, who loves food. She is funny, but terribly obsessive. Monica was overweight as a child, and as an adult she has become a perfectionist.* Marilyn Monroe is often seen as a tragic figure, who despite great beauty and a voluptuous figure, was unable to find true love and happiness. Diana, Princess of Wales, has been linked since her death with almost mythical goodness or charity, but also with psychological problems and eating disorders.

we can invite anyone we want into our dreams

112

* The only male character in the dream is Frank Sinatra, who is singing but being ignored. He is another legend of our age but has some questionable associations, in his case with the criminal underworld. Finally, we should not forget the dreamer who is present in the dream but is passively watching the activity of the other dream characters. She feels honored to be among them.

New York
New York

* *From the initial description of the "personalities" in this dream we can see that, on the negative side, two of the characters, Monica and Princess Diana, are associated with food, obsessive behavior, and eating disorders. Two are associated with untimely death. One of them, Marilyn Monroe, is known for her full figure and beauty. It may be important that the "fuller figure" is arguing with the cook!*

I contain multitudes

Fritz Perls says that every object, character, setting, and feeling in a dream is part of the dreamer. The idea is that our personalities are made up of many components, or sub-personalities, that are, in and of themselves, autonomous.

might the food theme be the connection between these famous people?

the Gestalt
empty chair

It could be me

Another approach to dreams about famous people is that they show aspects of ourselves that we aspire to. In the example dream, perhaps the positive attributes of each of the characters are what the dreamer aspires to be like. Or perhaps such dreams reveal characteristics that have been long overlooked by the dreamer but which she possesses, for example, a talent for singing. Alternately, perhaps the dreamer has a need for personal recognition that isn't being realized during waking, so fame is the main theme of her dreams, thus fulfilling a wish. Her unconscious may have projected the fame onto other dream characters to disguise the wish in herself.

IT'S AN HONOR

✱ If I were working with this dream I would ask the dreamer to enter into a dialogue with the characters using the GESTALT EMPTY CHAIR TECHNIQUE. It would also be a good idea for her to explore her attitude toward her body.

✱ It is also important to note that on some level the dreamer is "HONORED" by the presence of these parts of herself. The use of this word is important. She didn't

I feel so honored

the company of famous people can
have a humbling effect

Where for psychoanalysts dreams are the "royal road to the unconscious," to Gestalt practitioners they are the "royal road to integration."

Petruska Clarkson, 1995

say "pleased," or "pleasantly surprised"; she specifically used the word "honored." There are several meanings for the word:

being a person of honor; the honor of winning a battle; honor is at stake; protecting a lady's honor; being a hero treated with honor; and being honored to serve a person.

knight in shining armor

This tends to suggest that the dream is a message relating to being true to the dreamer's self—honoring the part of her that knows she is in trouble.

* *This dream highlighted a problem in the dreamer's life. Although different interpretations are suggested here, the idea that dreams reflect neurosis or psychological distress is essentially Freudian. This dream was actually recollected by a person in the course of therapy. She confirmed the concerns outlined here, was recommended to an appropriate eating disorders specialist, and is now doing fine.*

WHAT DOES IT MEAN?

Gayle Delaney points out that there are multiple meanings to dreams containing famous people. While psychoanalytic theory tends to say that older famous male and female characters are actually the dreamer's parents, Jungians may say that in some dreams famous people show an inflated ego. It is probably best not to form a judgment about these ideas until the dreamer can verify the interpretation.

parents are always appearing in dreams in one guise or another

115

THEME 6: ANIMALS IN DREAMS

* There are many interpretations of what animals may represent in dreams. One interpretation technique involves keeping a dream journal. Select an animal that keeps recurring in the dreams; then select all the dreams containing it. Then identify the overarching theme in each dream.

insects might represent petty irritations

Bugs and insects

They can represent small irritating things that "bug" the dreamer. In the case of ants and bees bugs may also indicate community, or working closely with others.

WHAT SORT OF ANIMAL?

* It can help if each dream is given a title that summarizes what the dream is about. Look at the setting, the feelings that arise, and the context in which the animal appears. Then try to understand the dreams as a related story. You will find the results both fascinating and revealing.

* **Dogs:** In Western culture dogs are often described as "man's best friend." The appearance of a dog in a dream can mean loyalty and friendship. Depending on the feelings that accompany the dream, dogs can indicate either a growing strength in a friendship; or the opposite, that the friendship is in trouble.

* **Cats:** Cats tend to represent the feminine. If the cat is a domestic cat then it may link to cultural expectations of the female, showing behaviors that are learned as part of our expected roles, becoming domesticated so to speak. But if the cat is wild then it tends to indicate strong feminine energies that remain untamed. Cats can also signify independence.

116

it might bite

Freud's patient little
Hans was afraid of
horses in his dreams

★ **Eagles:** Associated with that which soars. The dreamer might see himself as higher than others, or the dream might show the raising of spiritual awareness and vision. The opposite of feeling above others is to feel inferior. Perhaps the person is compensating for this in the dream.

★ **Pigs:** Not a favorite animal in our culture. Eating its flesh is forbidden for Jews and Muslims, so there are links with being dirty and unfit for consumption. It can show a poor diet, or greed. It can also be a metaphor for being "pig-headed"—either in the dreamer, or someone close.

★ **Horses:** A complicated symbol with many meanings, depending on the type and color of the horse, and its context. For example, the horse is a beast of burden, and one of the most badly treated of all animals, so it can represent being put upon. If the horse is a stallion it may be linked to sexuality. One of Freud's most famous dream analyses featured a horse.

FREUD AND LITTLE HANS

Hans developed a phobia of horses when he was 5 years old. He was afraid that they would bite him. He was most afraid of white horses that wore blinkers. A series of letters passed between Freud and Hans's father. Freud concluded that the horse in Hans's dreams symbolized his father. The boy desired his mother. The child's fear that the horse would bite him symbolized his fear that his father would castrate him in punishment for his incestuous feelings toward his mother. Hans's father had pale skin and wore glasses that could have resembled the blinkers worn by horses. When his father talked to him and reassured him, he overcame his fear.

INTERPRETING ANIMAL DREAMS

✳ Rosemary Guiley believes that animal dreams are some of the most revealing about the emotional, psychological, and physical state of the dreamer. They tell us about the instinctual or primitive parts of ourselves. *For example, Guiley explains that if we dream of neglecting an animal, it can show that we are neglecting parts of our own lives. Which parts? The key to understanding this lies in understanding what the animal represents.*

✳ Perhaps one of the most frequently reported "animals" in dreams is the snake. It doesn't take much imagination to come up with a Freudian interpretation for this symbol—the <u>PHALLUS</u>. But this explanation alone doesn't do the symbol justice. In Greek mythology the snake represents healing, which can be spiritual, emotional, psychological, or physical.

dreaming about a snake in the grass may mean you need to be wary

children have lots
of animal dreams

Animals and gender

One finding that was consistent for both girls and boys is that if an animal appears in a dream it is usually the main character, not one that stays in the background. Girls dream more about pets, while boys dream more of untamed native animals. In adult dreams, when animals do appear, they are dangerous creatures with which the dreamer interacts aggressively.

CHILDREN'S DREAMS

Research into children's dreams shows that they contain significantly more references to animals than are present in adults' dreams. Swiss researcher Inge Strauch describes the types of animals that children dream about:

	Girls	Boys
Pets	41.7%	22.2%
Barnyard animals	21.4%	16.7%
Native animals	28.6%	38.9%
Exotic animals	8.3%	22.2%

✱ There is also the "snake in the grass"— the snake may show that someone close isn't trustworthy. *In archetypal terms, Jung says that the snake represents transformation, change, and possibly God.* In keeping with his ideas about balance he said that the snake could also have negative connotations. So girls tend to dream about their pets while boys dream of exotic animals.

"Snakes are primitive and cold blooded [and] symbolize the instinctual side of the unconscious."
Carl Jung

THEME 7: DREAMS OF FALLING

* Nearly everybody reports having dreamed of falling at some time or other. However, an important distinction needs to be made between two types of "falling" experience related to sleep.

Prediction?

Ann Faraday says we should look at the predictive nature of the dream. Is there any possibility that the next day there will be a fall or accident of some kind? She recommends checking things such as climbing equipment. Otherwise, falling dreams may signify loss of face, or failing to meet the expectation of others in some way.

falling might suggest a loss of control

falling dreams might be a warning of a slip to come

DROPPING OFF

* Many people feel that they are falling as they drop off to sleep. This type of "dream" often results in vivid feelings of falling, and then a jolt as the person comes back into consciousness. This type of falling is associated with the descent into sleep. It is generally agreed that it has no psychological meaning. Rather, it is part of the process of letting go of consciousness.

* A common myth exists regarding this phenomenon: the belief that if the sleeper hits the floor they will die. However, there is also the "real" falling dream. This happens once sleep has been initiated, is accompanied by visual imagery, and contains a storyline. This is a "true dream" and can be looked at in terms of psychological meaning.

a falling dream might mean a loss of respect

UNPLEASANT STUFF

* *Dreams of falling are usually reported as unpleasant experiences. Several interpretations seem to appear regularly in the literature about dreaming. For example, Robert Van de Castle says they represent the fall from grace, the descent into hell, or some kind of loss of status, respect, or control.*

* Gayle Delaney, on the other hand, suggests that what is occurring in the dream prior to the fall is important. This can give clues as to which area of life the dreamer fears "falling down" in. For example, if the dreamer reports being at driver's school, learning to drive, then it might mean he is anxious about passing his driving test.

FALLING FROM GRACE

If we look at a saying related to falling, we remember that "pride goes before a fall"; it may be for some of us that we are being the top dog, and the underdog is trying to warn us against having a superior attitude.

pride goes before a fall

121

NICE FALLING DREAMS

✱ What about when falling dreams are nice? Occasionally, the dreamer may report a wonderful dream full of vivid images, including pleasant feelings of falling and finding themselves landing on a bed of soft feathers or flowers. This can represent "FALLING BACK TO EARTH." Maybe the person hasn't felt grounded in her life, or has had her head in the clouds about some venture or project. In this case the dream shows a return to reality.

pleasant falling dreams are associated with coming back to firm ground

✱ Researchers who have investigated typical or universal dreams have found that as many as 87% of people have dreamed of falling at least once. There is also some indication that this type of dream is culturally universal. Three hundred South African Bushmen were asked if they had falling dreams, and most said they had. However, the context in which the falling occurred was different from the setting reported by Americans.

✳ The Bushmen had no experience of flight or high buildings. Instead, they reported falling into wells or pits. This seems to suggest that there may be universal feelings in dreams, but that the setting or context in which they take place is determined by the person's waking surroundings. This supports to some extent Calvin Hall's continuity hypothesis.

falling might be an expression of fear

Fear

Freud also says that falling dreams can be an expression of fear, or reflect a time when as a child the dreamer fell, from bed or some other place. So in their simplest form they can be an actual memory that has been reawakened from the past some time during the previous day.

it's very unlikely that a falling dream would end with your falling out of bed

strange contraption

THEME 8: DREAMS OF FLYING

* "I was having a dream and suddenly I started to fly. I just put out my arms and it happened. I wasn't afraid anymore. Everything was so peaceful and I knew everything. It was so incredibly beautiful. I could control going up and down, my

overcoming difficulties might be the meaning behind a flying dream

speed—everything. It was so real. I looked at the sky; it was blue and clear. I was flying and I felt very happy."

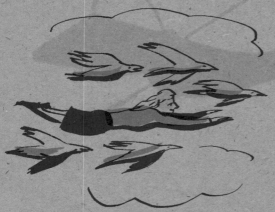

EUPHORIA

flying dreams are nearly always joyful

* This dream is in sharp contrast with falling dreams. The main elements of flying dreams are positive emotions, even euphoria, at being able to fly, and a sense of control or achievement. There

LUCID DREAMING

This occurs when you become aware while still in the dream that you are dreaming. Approximately 60% of people report having a lucid dream at least once. They are most common in late adolescence. In some instances people can even control the way the dream unfolds —though one of the paradoxes of lucid dreams is that if people try to do this too hard they wake up!

is sometimes a sense of beauty, or of being at one with nature. *Flying in a dream often happens just before the dream becomes lucid.*

✳ Anthony Shafton writes that he has found 24 different motifs, or meanings, for flying dreams. He says they can be interpreted as anything from prodromal dreams showing physical illness (for example, vestibular infection, or stimulation), to the paranormal, including out-of-body experiences and astral projection. More psychological interpretations include infantile grandiosity, a will to dominate, and rising above difficulties.

the child's sense of security as it leaps into its parent's arms might be re-created in a flying dream

Freud and flying

Freud believed that there were several possible causes of flying dreams. First, they could be memories of playing retrieved from childhood. One of the games that children love to play involve running across a room, or jumping off a box, and being caught by an adult. The child knows that she will be caught, so feels safe to jump. Flying dreams are re-creations of this blissful state. However—not to move too far from the sexual connotations expected from Freud—flying dreams in men could be symbols for an erect phallus, and in women could show the unconscious desire for a penis.

125

a flying dream might show a
desire to escape from a
difficult situation

Where there's hope

Because of the intense positive feelings that accompany many flying dreams, many of the interpretations are hopeful. It may be that such dreams show the dreamer his ability to rise above a situation and look down upon it. Flying can also show that the dreamer feels a sense of power or accomplishment, and may occur immediately after the completion of an important project. Delia Cushway and Robyn Sewell believe that flying dreams show that the dreamer has mastered a situation in life.

PSYCHOLOGICAL INTERPRETATIONS

✱ *Ann Faraday says that flying dreams rarely have literal meaning, so we must look to the psychological to understand them. She agrees that they are usually enjoyable, but also points out that the dreamer can fly away from a threat in*

a sense of
achievement at
completing a task
could produce a
flying dream

the dream environment. When this happens the dreamer usually awakens in terror. She says that this type of occurrence shows the dreamer that some situation that he feels in control of when he is awake is actually starting to "fly away from him." Often, the situation is one involving an emotional investment for the dreamer.

WHY THIS DREAM?

✱ Gayle Delaney suggests that dreamers should pay close attention to details in their dreams. They should ask themselves, when they wake, why they have had this dream at this time. Is there a life issue that may have lead to this dream? Do they feel they are about to have a breakthrough in any area?

you must be fully prepared before takeoff

HOW HIGH CAN YOU GO?

One thing that may be important is the height the dreamer is flying at. If they only go so high, or run into obstacles or problems, this could show that their goals are set too high. Sometimes it is best to stay where we are, rather than fly off without being fully prepared. This may be the time to revise any plans.

flying suggests a desire for freedom

127

THEME 9: DREAMS OF THE DEAD

* As well as looking at the effect that a dream interpretation can have on waking life, we can look at the reverse effect that a life situation can have on dream content. The relationship between dreams and waking is not one way, but a reciprocal process where sleep affects waking, and waking affects sleep. One life event that can be looked at in this way is the death of a loved one, and how a person's dreams reflect how he or she is dealing with this.

But how did I die?

GRIEF AND DREAMS

* The dreams that we have after the death of a loved one show, in a way that no other type of dream can, just how truthful dreams are at representing our ability to adapt to situations in our lives. As the stages of grieving evolve, dream

RELOCATION

Garfield says that dreams after a death help the dreamer to pass through the "four tasks of grief." These are: to accept the reality of the loss; to experience the pain of losing someone; to adjust to the environment without the person; and to "emotionally relocate." Grief dreams help the dreamer to adjust to the death of a loved one, and to carry on after he is gone.

the death of a loved one is likely to stimulate dreams

content changes accordingly. The dreams we have immediately after someone dies are very different from those we have months or years later.

✱ One of the best studies that describes these changes was conducted by **Deirdre Barratt**. She analyzed over 1,400 "grief dreams" and found that four distinct stages emerge, each corresponding to a waking stage in the grief process.

STAGE ONE: BACK-TO-LIFE DREAMS

✱ These dreams begin almost immediately after a death and continue for several months. They occur most commonly some 3 months after the death. In the dream the dead person comes back to life and often wants to discuss the circumstances surrounding his death. The dreamer may find the dream distressing or be comforted by the dead person's presence. Sometimes the deceased is seen as a corpse that moves a finger or opens its eyes to show the dreamer he isn't dead and it's all been a terrible mistake.

✱ *These dreams represent denial of death, and occasionally show that the dreamer feels guilt over the death. The dreamer's relationship with the dead person may have been very close. During waking she may feel shocked, and be trying to come to terms with the death, and her feelings of guilt.*

a dream might reflect a wish to say goodbye to the dead person

A LEAVE-TAKING DREAM

"I saw my father standing in a doorway. I said, 'What are you doing here? I thought you were dead.' He replies, 'I just came to say goodbye and tell you I'm fine. They are looking after me really well in here.' He points to the door. I feel a great surge of love, and relief. I know I can relax now. That he is OK."

sometimes technology
helps us contact the
dead in dreams

What is death like?

*Another characteristic of
this type of dream is that
the dreamer often asks the
person what it is like to
be dead, and the dead
person is evasive in his
answer. This suggests that
one of the main meanings
of state-of-death dreams is
that the dreamer has
concerns about her own
mortality, which she
projects onto someone
who she knows
has already died.*

we want to know what
happens after death

STAGE TWO: ADVICE DREAMS

✱ The next stage that emerges involves the dead person appearing as if he is alive and has come back to offer advice to the dreamer, who often feels comforted. This type of dream is often experienced as if it foretells an event, and because of this has been associated with PRECOGNITION. Although there are lots of anecdotal reports of precognition in this type of dream, there is no research showing whether the information the dead person relays actually comes to pass in the dreamer's life.

✱ *This type of dream usually shows the waking concerns of the dreamer, and may indicate ways that the dead person helped them when he or she was alive. As in back-to-life dreams, the dreamer has usually shared a close relationship with the person who has died. Advice dreams happen between 2 months and 10 years after the person has died, but on average about 3 years after death—after the initial shock has worn off, and when the dreamer is actively grieving for his or her loss.*

STAGE THREE: LEAVE-TAKING DREAMS

✱ In leave-taking dreams the dead person is going somewhere and returns to say goodbye. These dreams occur between 8 months and 12 years after the death—commonly 3 years. The feelings that accompany these dreams are usually pleasant and comforting. The dreamer often reports that the dream helped him or her to come to terms with the death.

✳ Dreams of this sort show that the dreamer has begun to accept the passing of the dead person. The feelings are usually pleasant, and the dreamer reports a sense of relief. Interestingly, in Barratt's study 11% of these dreams were lucid. Lucid dreams are often reported as very positive experiences and can be associated with spiritual growth.

STAGE FOUR: STATE-OF-DEATH DREAMS

✳ As the name suggests, in this type of dream the person who died in "real life" is also dead in the dreams. These dreams can be pleasant or unpleasant, and can be very disturbing. To have this type of dream the dreamer doesn't have to know the dead person well, he might just be acquainted with her. The actual death is often reported as having been sudden, most commonly in an accident.

✳ This type of dream can occur a long time after the person's death. In Barratt's study the earliest was reported just 4 months after the person had died, but the majority occurred 5 years after the death. In 23% of the dreams the dead person communicated by telephone. If we compare this percentage with other typical dreams, telephones are only mentioned in about 3% of dreams.

Useful study

One of the most useful things about studies of this type is that it helps us to know what to expect when we lose someone. It is common to dream about a person when he or she has died, but it can be very distressing the first time it happens. Many people who go into grief counseling report dreams of this type, and it may help them to know that these dreams are part of the natural process of grieving.

dreams are part of the grieving process

131

THEME 10: DREAMS OF BEING DEAD OR DYING

* What about dreams that feature death, but no one has died? There can be dreams in which either the dreamer or someone close to her dies, although she or he is not dead in waking reality. "I am walking with my mother in a garden filled with beautiful flowers. I can smell their fragrance in the air. I feel calm and at peace. Suddenly my mother falls to the ground. I realize she isn't breathing. I cry for someone to help me, and see strangers running toward me, to help. They take over, and I notice the flowers have lost their luster and are now tinged with decay. I see new growth sprouting from the flowerbed. I sadly realize that nothing lives forever. I wake up feeling very sad and shaken."

MOVING ON

* This dream described above happened during a TRANSITION POINT in the dreamer's life. At that time, although she had nursed many people who were dying, she had never lost anyone very close to her, and it was a fear of hers. She had also made the decision to leave this line of work and explore another path. She felt afraid of the future.

* *How would some past and present analysts interpret this dream?* Freud would say that she had a wish for her

Killing parents

Sometimes people dream of killing their parents. Freud would say this symbolized the Oedipus complex, while a Jungian interpretation might be that such dreams show a major archetypal process where the dreamer is symbolically attempting to separate from his or her parent's attitudes.

mother to die! This wish might originate in childhood. The dreamer has successfully hidden the wish in the sadness and panic she reports when her mother collapsed. She even diverts attention away from the wish by including some characters that can help to bring her mother back to life. But she wakes before this occurs, and she even accepts the loss on some level.

dying in dreams often symbolizes a change of lifestyle

A new way of life

Jeremy Taylor, a Jungian analyst, is quite specific about the meaning of this type of dream. He says: "When death appears in a dream, it is always associated with the growth and development of the personality or character." *He states that it can be the death of an attitude, old behavior, or way of thinking. If the way the person dies is long and protracted, this can symbolize how painful and difficult some changes can be.*

dreams of death remind us of our mortality

✱ Thus death dreams suggest a transformation in some arena of the dreamer's life. The way the person (or animal) dies can show the degree to which the dreamer is willing to get rid of some aspect of his or her life and move on.

death dreams reveal a fear of loss

goodbye cruel world

suicide dreams don't
mean that the person
actually wants to
kill themselves

SUICIDE DREAMS

✱ Jeremy Taylor also comments on
SUICIDE in dreams. When the dreamer
takes his own life this may be an
analogy for "wanting to end it all." The
dreamer should ask himself which area
of his life he feels like this about. It
doesn't mean that the person actually
wants to kill himself.

✱ The example dream described at
the beginning of this section is close to
Jeremy Taylor's interpretation. The
dreamer was about to leave an old way
of life and begin a new one. There is
also an element of continuity in as
much as she was concerned about how
she would react if one of her loved
ones died. At the time she had been
working with the elderly for 10 years.

take it as
a warning

* When asked to describe her relationship with her clients she said that when she cared for the elderly she always remembered that they were someone else's mother or father. Her guilt at leaving was dealt with by cleverly reproduced new workers who would come in and take over for her in the role of helper. She is reminded to keep in mind that no one is indispensable.

* The reality of death is depicted; the truth is that no one lives forever. The "death" of her old job (flowers) is also what the new growth builds upon (the new shoots). This is true, because we often use our past experiences to help us understand new ones.

death dreams can be very disturbing

The real thing?

Ann Faraday's interpretation is in some agreement with Freud's. She says death dreams can show resentment toward the people who are dead or dying. In some ways the who, why, and wherefore aren't important. Dreams of death usually allow us to express sadness, perhaps not normally acknowledged. They let the dreamer express emotions that have been repressed, and provide a scenario where these emotions can be played out. Alternately, if we dream that our partner has died, this can show that we feel we are becoming distant from him or her, and allow us to accept the abandonment that we feel.

phew, you're still alive

dreaming about your partner's death may be a sign that you feel distant from them

THEME 11: DREAMS OF GIVING BIRTH

* "I felt as if I had been in labor forever. I pushed and pushed but felt like I was getting nowhere. Time seemed to stand still. I gave one final huge push and my baby was born. When I looked at it, it seemed very small. I hadn't realized it would be so hard."

A MAJOR EVENT

Conception and birth are driven by a biological imperative to reproduce. The transition from having no responsibilities to being a parent is one of the most important that we will make in our lifetime. It is hardly surprising that this state influences our dreams.

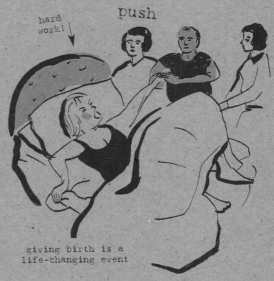

hard work!

push

giving birth is a
life-changing event

pregnancy now
not just
for women

HAPPY BIRTHDAY

* Where a death dream heralds the end of a cycle, dreaming of a birth shows the beginning of a new one. *Both events are truly universal, everybody will experience both, and so they are marked by rites in every culture.* Birth dreams, as you might expect, are most commonly reported by women, yet are not a purely female phenomenon; men also report having them. This suggests that the notion of giving birth has been internalized, symbolizing life issues, and has psychological connotations other than the literal meaning of bearing children. *Some of the possible meanings will come as no surprise. For example, new beginnings, the end of one cycle and the beginning of another, or the development of a project of some sort. Perhaps even the birth of a new awareness.*

✳ this a completely new idea ☆

dreaming of birth can mean the start of a new project

the birth of a child affects the whole family

✳ Let us consider what a dream about birth actually entails. Babies don't just arrive in the world. The reason the birth process is called <u>LABOR</u> is because it is such hard work. Labor can last for many hours, and the birth is just the final stage in a long process, beginning at the moment of conception. In many cases, to dream of a birth also shows the hard work that goes into the development and appearance of a "new project."

NEW VENTURES

Gayle Delaney says that men who have had labor or pregnancy dreams tend to relate to the conception of an idea that results in the birth of a new business venture. The length of the pregnancy may give an indication of when the idea or project was conceived, and for how long it has been maturing.

what is the future going to bring?

Practicing for the future

Alan Seigel has looked at the impact of actual pregnancy on the dreams of both the mother and the father. He found that women who have threatening dreams during pregnancy have safer and shorter labors! It is also common for women to have dreams about the safety of their partners during pregnancy, but it seems that women who have these dreams are good at dealing with conflict. Research in this area tends to suggest an adaptive function for dreaming. It is almost as if the sleeping brain is presenting the dreamer with many possible scenarios, which they are able to rehearse and then use in their waking life.

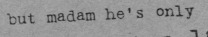

but madam he's only
10 minutes late

pregnant women often
dream of their
partners' safety

THE FREUDIAN VIEW

* *Freud believed that dreams about giving birth are often hidden in other dream images. For example, a bird bringing a gift, or the dreamer receiving a message might symbolically be suggestive of birth.*

* One of the criticisms that has been made against Freud's theory regarding his idea about disguised symbols applies here. The argument

what is the
message?

a man's dream of being pregnant might suggest his fear of being left out

goes something like this: The wish that is embedded in the dream is so damaging to the dreamer that it is hidden from him or her in the objects present in the dream. But if this is true, then why are some of the symbols so obvious, why aren't the meanings more difficult to access? There are few people in our culture who wouldn't recognize that a "bird bringing a gift" was a metaphor for a birth. Does this argument make some of Freud's ideas redundant?

✱ Another distinction is necessary. So far we have spoken about new births, but what if the dream is about rebirth? In archetypal terms this is a BIG DREAM. Jung was particularly interested in looking at the relationship between dreams, organized religion, and myths. *The birth dream is an archetype of the Christian belief that if we are good and work hard we will go to heaven.* Jung believed that birth dreams could also show the birth of a new part of the personality, which moved the individual close to the process of INDIVIDUATION (see page 78). He suggested that when the dream appeared was important, as it might show where the dreamer was in the individuation process.

Male pregnancy

Dream researchers know that it is notoriously difficult to get men to take part in dream research. Despite this obstacle, Seigel shows that, contrary to current stereotypes, men experience powerful emotional feelings about becoming fathers, and these concerns show up in their dreams. One of the themes is a fear that they will be left out when the baby arrives. They also report sympathy-labor dreams, where they are actually pregnant and having the baby. They also report increased sexual adventure dreams— possibly a last reminder for the unconscious that the time for "sowing wild oats" is over.

cars represent the
dreamer's mind

Which transport?

Cars represent the
dreamer's personality
and the state of the
unconscious mind.
*What kind of car is it?
Who is the driver?*
The boat is a symbol
for the body, the vehicle
that carries the person
through life. It can also
represent the feminine
womb. In Egyptian
times it was the
boatman who carried
the soul to the
underworld.
Trains: Many
factors influence the
interpretation of train
dreams. *What kind of
train is it? What kind
of track or station? Is
the train going off into
the distance? Is it above
or below the ground?*

boats are a symbol
of the body

THEME 12: TRAINS, PLANES, AND AUTOMOBILES

✻ "I rush to the station and buy
a ticket for the next train. I am
aware that I am late and will have
to rush to catch it. I manage to get
to the platform only to see the
train pulling out without me. I am
left feeling really anxious and
frustrated."

I'm going to the
underworld

did Egyptians
dream about
missing the boat?

ON THE MOVE

✻ Trains are a relatively recent invention; in
terms of past eras and the universality of
dream themes, we might wonder if people
through history have dreamed of missing
the boat, horse, or whatever mode of
transportation was familiar.

the train now leaving

missing the train might suggest worry about the pace of life

THE PLANE

Planes are the modern, technological version of the bird. They represent or reflect someone who aspires to freedom. At what speed do you like to travel through life? Are you in a jet or in a glider?

I'm as free as a bird

airplanes represent freedom

★ More seriously, there are several ways in which we can travel in dreams, each of which says something about our personality. If public transportation is reported in a dream it is an indication of the social links we form in our journey through life. Trains, for example, are a very organized mode of travel. The train station is a place where we arrive, wait, and depart. *Railroads form part of a much larger network, and trains are subject to strict timetables. Traveling by train involves handing over control of the journey to others. Most researchers see trains as symbolic of the way a dreamer is moving through life.*

JUNG VS. FREUD

✱ Jungian analysts say that dreams where travel or trains are involved show the person's progression in the process of <u>INDIVIDUATION</u>. However, Freud says that travel dreams are symbolic of the death instinct, <u>THANATOS</u>, and may be premonitory of death. In fact, some psychoanalysts have taken them as indications of suicidal tendencies. On a more positive note we need have no fear of this in the example dream, because the dreamer missed the train. *So in Freudian terms they have fulfilled their wish to stay alive and have missed, narrowly in this case, getting on the train for their last journey!*

✱ So many people have had dreams in which they catch a train, the death-wish interpretation must be in some doubt. Instead we can turn to the symbolic nature of the train. It is reminiscent of the phallus, and if the train goes into a tunnel this would be a classic case of a <u>WISH-FULFILLMENT DREAM</u> for intercourse. Did our unfortunate dreamer,

KEY WORDS

THANATOS:
This refers to one of the main life forces in Freudian theory. It represents the death energy or destructive side of man. It needs to be expressed, or we may turn it upon ourselves.

LIBIDO:
The sexual instinct, the stronger and more important of the two motivating life forces.

✱ yes!
I missed
the boat

missing the boat
might mean
fulfilling a wish
to stay alive

busy people who travel
a lot are likely to
dream about traveling

trains have lots of
obvious meanings

in missing the train, also miss the
alternative Freudian interpretation of
a sexual opportunity?

A BLOW FOR
COMMON SENSE

✶ Finally, and perhaps the most
common-sense interpretation of all, is
that people who usually have dreams
where they miss trains, or other forms
of transportation, are usually quite
successful, ruled by their appointment
books, and travel a lot. This suggests
an element of continuity with waking
life. *The dream may simply be a
representation of anxiety, or of the
dreamer's feeling that she has "missed
the boat" in some area of her life.*

Missing an opportunity

*Ann Faraday suggests
that the dreamer look
inside to the looking-
glass self, to find the
"secret saboteur." Which
part of him doesn't want
to catch some of the
opportunities that present
themselves? She suggests
using the empty chair
technique and talking to
this part of himself. Ask
what was on the train,
and why the dreamer
unconsciously wished not
to catch it.*

what does this dream
say about you?

THEME 13: DREAMS OF BEING PHYSICALLY ATTACKED

* In a study of typical dreams conducted in 1961 by Ward, Beck, and Rascoe, it was found that being attacked was the most common dream people mentioned. The attacker can appear in many forms, some of which are discussed in Theme 14 and Theme 15: creatures, monsters, and mythical beasts.

KEY WORDS

FREUD'S ELEMENTS OF PERSONALITY
THE ID: The wild part of the self, it requires instant gratification. Not logically but biologically motivated.
THE EGO: The part of us that tries to maintain equilibrium, holding the other elements of the personality together. The cognitive or psychological aspect of the personality.
THE SUPEREGO: This is experienced as the person's conscience, and is usually based on family values. It is the social aspect of the personality, and may appear in dreams as the attacker.

psychological monsters can attack us in dreams

UNDER THREAT

* Calvin Hall analyzed the content of dreams where the dreamer was attacked, and found that a human attacker was nearly always male. *In many cases the dreamer reported that the attack was unprovoked.* However, another common occurrence was that the attacker was a ferocious animal. Further research has shown that as the level of aggression in

being chased
is a common
anxiety dream

dreams increases, so do the reported numbers of animals. This has lead to the conclusion that animals can often stand for threats in the dreamer's life.

* *The general recurring elements of attack dreams are that in response to the attack or threat the dreamer runs away, and this often leads to the perception of being chased (see Theme 14). Hall concluded from this that people who dream of being attacked had "weak, passive, inferior, or helpless" senses of self when they had the dream.*

* Robert Van de Castle, one of Hall's coworkers, is less harsh, and suggests that attack dreams are anxiety dreams. It may be that dreamers project onto other dream characters threats they may unconsciously sense in their waking life from people near them (or from a group of people).

Superego

If a series of attack dreams are experienced, it may be useful to ask what conflict there is in the waking life of the person. Is there unresolved conflict with someone known, for instance in their work environment? The dream setting may help determine where the waking conflict is. If after taking an honest look the dreamer fails to find any unresolved anger from others, then he should look at the state of his internal life. It may be that his Superego —the policeman of the personality—is being particularly punishing about some aspect of the dreamer's attitude or behavior, and is punishing the dreamer's ego during dreams.

I am your
superego

the superego is our
personal policeman

this is just what I wanted

aggressive dreams
might reflect a
need for love

More Freud

We can apply the Freudian idea of "reversal" to the dream. Being attacked may show a wish for a much more pleasant association. It also appears that if the dreamer is being "attacked" he or she does not wish to take responsibility for this, and leaves the initiation of the association to another dream character.

KEY WORDS

REVERSAL: This is a defense mechanism that transforms the symbol into its opposite to conceal its meaning from the dreamer, and make it difficult to establish.

WHO OR WHAT IS ATTACKING YOU?

✱ If a dream of being attacked is shared in a dream group—*for example, using Ullman's group work method*—the potential interpretations of such a dream become apparent. Everyone is afraid of being attacked by different "things," or has different vulnerabilities. When people are asked to share what the dream might mean "if this were my dream" there is an abundance of possible meanings.

it's a lion no, a monster a man-eater

group work will
bring out a range
of interpretations

AN OUTLET FOR AGGRESSION

✱ Jung's theory of COMPENSATION may be appropriate here. It may be that the dreamer is a pacifist, or has difficulty in

violence in the real world
often lessens the violence
of the dream world

Unresolved inner conflict

In Gestalt terms, the attack dream shows that the dreamer is in conflict with parts or a part of himself. In this case the dreamer should inquire into the nature of the attacker. What internal struggle is the dreamer representing in the dream? It may also be that the dreamer feels oppressed in some way; what is it he feels the need to fight for?

dealing with aggressive feelings, so these emotions manifest themselves in a dream. There is some research that supports this aspect of Jung's theory. For instance, aggressive dreams have been found to occur less frequently when the amount of violence in the dreamer's community increases.

✱ *It has also been recorded that Jewish men and women (who have historically been victimized in many societies) are frequently the recipients of unprovoked attacks during their dreams. This may indicate a link in the psyche of the community with its experiences, and supports Jung's idea of the existence of a collective consciousness.*

you look just like me

the dream might be
about warring
aspects of yourself

147

THEME 14: BEING CHASED, OR CHASING

* "I am in a dark place, running. I sense something behind me that is trying to catch me. I have great sense of urgency that I must get away from it. I suddenly find that I can't move, I feel very scared and realize that the thing is catching up with me."

it's coming
to get you

ON THE RUN

* There are many different versions of "being chased" in dreams, but the example dream contains many of the general elements. *Usually the person becomes aware in the dream of a threat or a person who wishes to harm him; then he starts running. At some point he may find that he is paralyzed, and cannot move.* When asked what feelings the dream contains he will report helplessness and intense fear.

the sense of fear after a chase dream can stay for some time

Recurring dreams

There is some evidence that "chase" dreams become recurring dreams, which are recalled at various times throughout the life span. They often begin in childhood, where most commonly the child is chased by a wild animal of some sort. However, as the person grows up the animal often transforms into a man or a group of men. These figures can often be recognized by their links to violence. For example they may present themselves as Nazis or as werewolves. They may have weapons or present some type of threat to the dreamer. Another manifestation of the hunter is a monster or demon of some sort.

✱ In evolutionary terms, and taking Jung's idea that we hold memories from previous civilizations and historical eras, these dreams may connect us to the part of ourselves that recalls being hunted. The physical nature of the dream, and the basic emotional content, support this idea. But there are also many psychological explanations.

oh no... not again

the chase dream might be part of our species memory of being hunted

✱ *Freud, for instance, would say that the dreamer is trying to fulfill a wish for a sexual encounter; rather than running from it, in reality he or she wishes to embrace it.*

✱ Another Jungian interpretation is that the dreamers are actually running from something in themselves; the thing that is pursuing them is a disassociated part of themselves that they want to avoid.

HOW COMMON ARE RECURRING DREAMS?

Ernest Hartmann, an expert on nightmares, carried out a study to find out how many American people had had recurring dreams and nightmares. His results showed this was a very common occurrence: 64% of women and 55% of men reported such dreams. A more recent study looking at British students has shown even higher percentages: 83% of women and 78% of men having had a recurring dream or nightmare at one time or another

these recurring dreams are so boring

recurring dreams are surprisingly common

THE HUNTER IMAGE

✱ If the Jungian interpretation fits for the dreamer, then he can explore the <u>HUNTER IMAGE</u> in more detail. He may be able to figure out what the image means, or what part of him it represents. He can then work toward acceptance of this aspect of himself. In Jungian terms this involves looking at the Shadow, and incorporating this part of himself so that a more balanced person emerges. All of us need to embrace the darker side of our natures. Not one of us is all good or all bad.

CONFRONT YOUR PURSUER

✱ *What if being chased has become a recurrent nightmare?* This can be very distressing for the dreamer. In this case we can look to one dream investigator who wrote extensively in the late 1800s about lucid dreams. **Hervey de Saint-Denys** suggested that you try to take active control of your dream and to confront what is chasing you. Ask it, "What do you want?" If you do this you will often find that the pursuer has something useful to tell you.

✱ *Another strategy would be to make the hunter slow down, or to transform it into an unthreatening image, so it no longer has any hold over you.*

SAINT-DENYS

Hervey de Saint-Denys lived in France and kept a dream journal from the age of 12 until his death. His notes contained nearly 2,000 entries. He is primarily known for his work with lucid dreams, developing the idea that lucidity can be used to overcome fears and nightmares. If we can control our dreams we can carry this control over into the waking world.

hello there dark side

we all need to find the darker side of our natures

face up to your
pursuer and find out
what it is

CONFRONTATION

The overwhelming message from the available interpretations is: Find out what is chasing you and confront it. If you can manage to do this you will find that the dream doesn't happen again. It has delivered its message.

* The dreaming mind CONSOLIDATES that which is feared, and makes it an image that can be recognized as a threat. The dreamer is not necessarily afraid of a person or a part of himself; it may be a situation or even an emotion that the dreamer is trying to avoid. If the dreamer manages to escape, this shows that he has a way out of the situation—*he just isn't aware of it yet.*

confrontation
might be better
than escape

THEME 15: MONSTERS, DEMONS, AND MYTHICAL CREATURES

* "I see the demon standing at the end of my bed. Looking at me. Everything is so real. It has red eyes and is horrible. It laughs, turns into vapor, and goes into my mouth. I can feel it inside my body, squirming."

MONSTERS FOR EVERYONE

There are literally hundreds of possible forms that mythical figures may take in dreams. They depend upon the culture that the dreamer lives in and the historical period when the dream occurs.

get lost!

our dream world can include various nasty monsters

meet my subpersonality

dream monsters can be aspects of our personality

CREATURES OF THE NIGHT

* It seems sensible after looking at chase dreams and what they mean to pay a little more attention to the often terrifying creatures we see in our dreams. *These images can be some of the most influential things in dreams.* Such powerful images: the good and the bad, the beautiful and the ugly. These true ARCHETYPAL IMAGES exist in all of us. Perhaps they show what Jung believed:

that we all have many possibilities, existing within us, all of them needing attention, and each of them having needs. We all have "parts of a whole," and our dreams give us the chance to meet, talk to, and interact with all these subpersonalities.

VIOLENT MONSTERS

∗ Freddie Kruger: The dream psychologist Kelly Bulkeley has written a wonderful essay on the appearance of modern-day demons in dreams and movies. He writes about **Freddie Kruger**, the alter ego that appears in a series of horror movies. He says that this image symbolizes the fear teenage boys feel about growing up. Freddie shows their fear of <u>IMPENDING ADULTHOOD AND SEXUALITY</u>, both of which appear terribly dangerous to young men.

∗ Werewolves: These are symbolic representations of fear, and the violence that is hiding in civilization. They are associated with the powers of darkness and the transformation of a person into a violent hunter. *Werewolves may be another symbol of the Jungian shadow.*

The shadow

The "shadow" has been discussed in previous interpretations. If an example of how the shadow may appear in dreams is required, then look out for dark, shadowy figures of either sex, not necessarily human. They may also be an animal or mythical creature of some kind. The point is that their presence results in bad feelings.

mysterious dark figures represent the shadow

153

children of the **night ha ha**

MYTHICAL FIGURES

✱ Vampires: Like the werewolf, vampires are associated with the "powers of darkness," but they are also PARASITES—creatures that live off others— and could therefore link with vicarious living, an area of life that is lived through another person, either emotionally or through that person's particular talent.

vampires take their life from other people

✱ The Goddess: In recent years numerous books have been written about finding the goddess within. She may appear in dreams as a beautiful woman with mysterious qualities. In one dream, the dreamer (who was male) was swimming with a woman who spoke to dolphins. She had magical attributes, and he believed that she represented the highest form of femininity that resided in his emotions (the water!).

✱ The Serpent: This is usually different from the average snake because of its size and sense of presence. *Its presence can indicate the need for healing in the psychological, physical, or spiritual arena*—possibly a part of the self that

SLEEP PARALYSIS

In a recent study looking at the content of sleep paralysis, more men and women reported "creatures" being present during the experience than is the case with normal dreaming. This ties in with the appearance of nighttime demons like incubi and succubi mentioned previously.

the dreamer doesn't want to face, for example, an addiction, or psychological harm caused by others.

✱ **The Angel:** In Judeo-Christian theology, angels are MESSENGERS sent from God. A dream angel is likely to represent a messenger from the highest parts of the self.

✱ **The Dragon:** This creature combines the serpent and the bird, and it is one of the great universal symbols. It can stand for hidden strength and wisdom. *Dragons can also symbolize the East, which in turn represents, according to Jung, the less logical and more holistic aspects of ourselves.*

angels bring messages from our noblest nature

VIVE LA DIFFERENCE

In a sample of 1,000 typical dreams, the total number of characters reported as imaginary creatures was 3% in men's and 7% in women's dreams. Characters can also change from one form to another in dreams.

you look different
tonight dear

monstrous figures might represent your secret feelings about someone close to you

dragons represent wisdom

HARTMANN'S THEORY

Hartmann proposes that the brain is a complex system. All the individual neurons in the brain connect with one another, forming networks. When they are activated, they produce thoughts, images, and consciousness. During waking the networks (or neurons) produce the types of associations that we connect with linear rational thought. During dreaming the connections are wider, producing broader, more bizarre imagery. However, this imagery is still based in the person's memory, and is influenced by his or her emotional state. Hartmann states that in this sense dreaming connects and contextualizes the dreamer's emotional experience. This is portrayed in the imagery we perceive as a dream.

THEME 16: THE DREAM SETTING OR LANDSCAPE

✴ There is a new theory about dream landscapes that states that the environment in which a dream takes place is important because it gives an overall impression of what the dream is about. It can set its mood, or emotional tone, and it can tell the dreamer which aspect of his or her life is being highlighted.

MAKING CONNECTIONS

✴ A discussion of dream landscapes forms a central part of **Ernest Hartmann's** theory about dreams. His ideas focus on how the brain works. Within his theory, the function of dreams is to make connections that are not possible in

dream landscapes show our emotional state

the waking brain. These connections are determined by the dreamer's EMOTIONAL CONCERNS. Hartmann argues that dream imagery is a METAPHOR for the dreamer's emotional state. In many cases, people don't dream of the event they are trying to deal with directly; instead their concerns are shown in the imagery of the dream. *If this theory is accepted, the importance of the dream setting becomes obvious.*

* *Hartmann's theory is useful because it presents ideas about how the dream is formed, as opposed to the previous theories, which are concerned with what dreams mean. If Hartmann's ideas are taken to their logical conclusion, they suggest that one of the main functions of dreaming is to provide an internal environment for the dreamer where he can experience and deal with emotions he may be having difficulty with while he is awake.*

* These ideas share some similarities with Freud's theory of DRIVE DISCHARGE. The influence goes back to Hartmann's own life; his father worked with Freud, and Hartmann recalls meeting him as a child. This theory is an improvement on Freud's WISH-FULFILLMENT function for dreams, portraying them as vehicles for emotional processing instead.

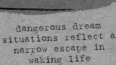

dangerous dream situations reflect a narrow escape in waking life

Traumatic dream settings

People who have just escaped from a life-threatening situation often report a dream environment with tidal waves or earthquakes. This contextualizes their terror. When people dream of accidents happening to people they love and are responsible for, this may contextualize their feelings of guilt about something.

157

Mountains

If the dream is at the top of a mountain, what goal has been, or is about to be, achieved? If the dream is about climbing a mountain, is the going getting heavy in some task or goal?

the kitchen is the creative room

HOUSES AND HOMES,

★ *If the house in the dream is one from the past, possibly childhood, it is important to ask what that place represents for the dreamer. What memories are associated with it; are they pleasant or unpleasant?* This type of setting also suggests an element of REGRESSION. In this case it would be important to look at what in the present has stimulated the memories of this past place.

★ Houses and homes are often associated with the people who live in them. Gayle Delaney states that in this case it is important to consider what it is about the person, and their home, that it has presented itself in the dream.

★ *What if the dream takes place in the dreamer's own home?* Homes are often symbolic of the internal state of the dreamer. It also helps to look at the state of repair the house is in. *Is it comfortable or does it need repairs or renovation?* A useful technique is to look at, and think about, what each room means to the dreamer. For example, the dreamer may have very different associations dependent upon whether he or she is in the kitchen or bedroom.

★ **The Kitchen:** In many homes this is the most CREATIVE room in the house. It is also at the heart of many families. *Explore what is "cooking" in the dreamer's life at the moment. And look at what part this room plays in family life.*

* **The Living Room:** This is the part of the house that is open to visitors, the room that often reflects who the people are who live in the house. In terms of Jung's theory this may be the PERSONA, or the social front. *What lies behind it? Are the people in this dream what they appear to be to the outside world?*

* **The Bedroom:** Often related to SEXUALITY, but in some cases people use sleep to avoid their problems, or to deprive themselves of the rest they need to be healthy.

* **The Bathroom:** The place of personal hygiene—*does the dreamer need to clean up his or her life in some way? Are there emotions that the dreamer needs to let go of, to flush away as it were?*

guns symbolize
conflict

The battlefield

This speaks for itself. Is there conflict in the person's environment? Who else is present, and what kind of weapons are being used? It may help to ask what cause is being fought for, and is it a good one?

CONTENT ANALYSIS BY SETTING

The setting in which a dream takes place is one of the major coding categories in Hall and Van de Castle's content analysis system. In their dream analyses they have shown that men's dreams tend to take place in a familiar outdoor setting. Conversely, women's dreams take place in a familiar indoor setting. For both men and women, the most common indoor setting is their home, followed by their workplace.

there are lots of possible different settings for dreams

159

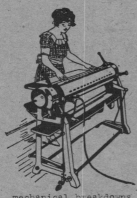

mechanical breakdowns
are often linked to
illness

KEY WORDS

PRODROMAL DREAMS:
Dreams that reflect
the dreamer's physical
state, and warn of
illness, disease, or
need for physical care.
This is an area of
dream research that is
becoming ever more
popular. Prodromal
dream studies have
investigated links
between dream
content and back
pain, breast lumps,
heart surgery, AIDS,
cancer, hysterectomy,
migraines, sore throat,
and other conditions.

THEME 17: MACHINES THAT DON'T WORK

✱ "I am driving my father's car. He takes very good care of it and it has never let him down. I am looking at the scenery that passes me and I approach a bridge. I put my foot on the brake to slow down, but nothing happens."

machines in dreams
are often linked to
our physical state

MY FATHER'S CAR

✱ This dream was reported by a women who had lost her father, very suddenly and unexpectedly. This is the first dream she recalled after his death, and although grief dreams have already been discussed, this dream portrays the meaning that cars, machinery, and other technological breakdowns can have for the dreamer.

★ *The dream is a literal representation of the dreamer's distress at the loss of her father. When questioned she said that his car was the "thing" that she most associated with him. He would never have let her drive it, and he was fanatical about getting it serviced. Although his death was sudden and unexpected, in retrospect there were hints that he was ill, but he didn't pursue the symptoms. The main feeling she had about his death was: How could he take so much care of everything else (the car) and leave out himself!*

A WARNING

★ There is considerable research that looks at dreams and the onset of illness. It suggests that changes in physical state may be picked up by the dreaming brain before they are consciously perceived.

One of the areas that has been studied is dreams collected prior to surgery. Researchers found that before an operation people dreamed of images that were linked to their particular physiological problem. For example, people about to have arterial heart surgery reported dreaming of having pipes cleaned in their house.

Get a checkup

The idea that in dreams, machines and gadgets may be linked to the physical (bodily) self, is often talked about in relation to the idea of prodromal dreams. If a dream contains machinery that doesn't work, is out of control, is going too fast or too slow, or acts out of character, it is an indication that something is not quite right physically. It would be a good idea to explore what the images mean in terms of one's own physical state.

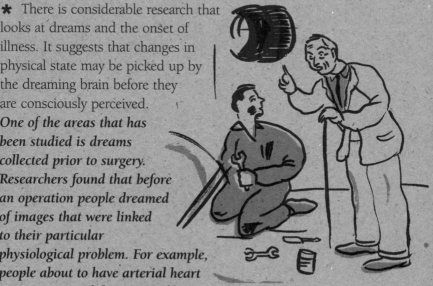

a dream about getting something fixed might relate to illness

161

Computers

With the rapid development of the computer generation, it will be interesting to see how computers emerge in dreams. One obvious analogy is to reverse the waking idea of the brain's being like a computer, and say that if a person dreams about a broken computer it may show that they are worried about their intellectual ability. Several students have reported dreams that feature computers. In most of them the main theme is "buying a new computer." This could possibly show that they want to buy or acquire a better brain, to help in their studies!

will dreams catch up
with the computer age?

everyday communicatio
problems will be
reflected in dreams

TRYING TO GET A MESSAGE THROUGH

✱ **What if the dreamer is trying to make an important telephone call and can't get through?** If the dream involves using a telephone, watching television or a movie, or reading books, this is an indication of trying to communicate with someone, something, or oneself.
So if there is a problem "getting through" or communicating in a dream, the dreamer should ask how this links to his waking life.
✱ Not surprisingly, women tend to dream more than men about HOUSEHOLD TECHNOLOGY—washing machines, stoves, and so on. It is possible that if the machines don't work, the woman is

expressing a wish to drop some of her gender role's expectations. If the "tools of her trade" are broken, the dream allows her to do this without taking responsibility for her dissatisfaction.

FREUD ONCE MORE

★ *Let's give the final word about machines that don't work to Freud. If a man dreams of machinery that doesn't work, and the machinery is a phallic symbol (car, gun, fountain pen) this indicates—as if you can't guess already —that the man is experiencing a loss of sexual energy or even impotence.*

some kinds of tools have phallic overtones

CYBERDREAMS

Technology has also begun to work for dreams. A huge dream community has developed over the Internet. This has bought dream work into the living room of each house with a computer. There are dream magazines, dream-sharing groups, dream art sites, and the possibility of downloading dream analysis tools to help understand your own dreams. The shared mission of most of these sites is to educate the larger community about the usefulness of dream exploration.

take that

if the machine does not work, you don't have to work

THEME 18: SWIMMING IN DREAMS, OR DREAMS CONTAINING WATER

* "I am swimming in clear, fresh water. It laps against my body. I feel calm, at peace."

FREUD AND WATER

Freud has said that swimming dreams could represent three things. First, the dreamer is, or was, a "bed wetter," and the dream shows the wish to return to the sensory pleasure of this act! Second, if the dreamer is swimming, this can show memories of being in the womb. Either of these dreams tend to show regression back to a childhood state, associated with being carefree and sensation-seeking beings. Third, it is possible that such a dream is a wish for sex with one's mother! This is because sex involves fluid exchange, and water in dreams apparently represents this.

swimming dreams can be very soothing

WATER, WATER EVERYWHERE

* Like other themes, dreams containing water can take many forms. *There are two main types: those where the dreamer is swimming in water and those in which other bodies of water feature.* These dreams can be either pleasant or unpleasant, and the activities in them may be very diverse. One common type is given in the example above.

* *The important elements of this type of dream are the state of the water (is it*

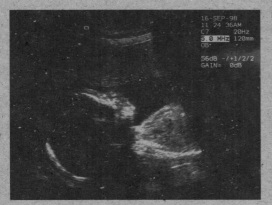

being buoyed up in a calm pool
of water might relate to
prebirth memories

Emotion

Another common interpretation of water in dreams is that it portrays emotion. Thus if the person dreams of a tidal wave, this shows that the dreamer has been holding back her anger or sadness, and is in danger of being overwhelmed by her emotions.

clean or dirty), the nature of the water (calm or stormy), and whether it is a man-made body of water or a natural sea, river, or ocean.

★ For Carl Jung, and most other Jungian analysts, water represents the UNCONSCIOUS. Thus, if the dreamer is swimming this can show that he or she is ready to dip into this part of the psyche.

the state of the
water reflects the
psychology of the
dreamer

Because water represents PSYCHIC ENERGY, the state of the water is very revealing. *If the water is calm and welcoming, so is the mental state of the dreamer; but a tempestuous and unpredictable character will have stormy dreams.*

she's doing the crawl

the carefree state of
childhood is suggested
by water dreams

and how does the
water feel?

water is an important
astrological feature

water is
essential to life

RIVERS OF LIFE

✴ Water is one of the ESSENTIAL ELEMENTS OF LIFE. Our bodies are made primarily of water, and while we can live without food for long periods, we die in a few days if we don't drink. For this reason there is something very fundamental about water appearing in dreams. If the dreamer sees steam it can represent her spirit or soul. For those who believe in ASTROLOGY there is also an association between water in dreams and the star sign Pisces.

✴ *Water has other religious and spiritual connotations. For example, in the Christian faith, water has very powerful* rituals associated with it. One of these is *baptism, where the sins of the person are washed away by immersion in water. If someone is in therapy and reports washing in water, this can be a sign that he or she is being cleansed of some emotion that has made him feel dirty or ashamed.*

✱ A water dream can also contain a warning. While too little water is life-threatening, so is too much of it. In the BIBLE, sending water is one of the chief ways in which God has shown his anger toward humans. ***Therefore a deluge of water can be interpreted as a punishment for something.*** This would need to be explored within the dreamer's life, and may be related to guilt of some kind. So there is much to be said for paying attention to the precise nature of the water and the dreamer during the dream.

I'm gonna wash away my sins

water has symbolic cleansing associations

A WORD OF CAUTION

Gayle Delaney thinks that there is no single meaning for water in a dream. She suggests that, as in many other typical dreams, there are many important factors to consider.

water is an ancient symbol of divine punishment

THEME 19: GOING TO THE BATHROOM IN DREAMS

* "I need to go to the bathroom, but no matter where I go there is no privacy. All the toilets I find are being used by someone and I am desperate to go, but can't find one anywhere. I feel embarrassed at the prospect of using one of these toilets."

TIME TO GO

* At one time or another nearly all of us have had a dream where we are in a bathroom, and want to either urinate or empty our bowels. *Many children experience such dreams.* In this case, and in the case of some adults' dreams, we are simply incorporating into our dream content a biological need to use the toilet.

your dream could be alerting you to a physical need

KEY WORDS

INCORPORATION: This refers to the inclusion in dream content of some actual physical stimulus in the environment. This phenomenon has been manipulated in several ways, by subjecting a sleeper to (for instance) sprays of water or ringing bells and seeing if this turns up in dream content after the dreamer has been awakened.

children frequently have toilet dreams

not being able to get
to the bathroom may
represent feelings of
frustration

HOW EMBARRASSING

✳ While the sleeping brain is sensitive to the internal state of the dreamer, and may represent physical needs in the form of dream content, there are also psychological explanations for these dreams. *The sample dream contains many of the main elements of "going to the bathroom dreams." The dreamer feels a sense of necessity. Searching for a safe, private place to go, he or she feels embarrassed at the prospect of having to do this in front of people. It is interesting to note that the toilets in the sample dream are occupied, by others "doing their business."*

169

But what does going to the bathroom represent in psychological terms? It is generally agreed that this shows a need to eliminate waste. It is getting rid of that which is no longer productive in a psychological, physical, or spiritual sense. It is also important to point out that if we are unable to eliminate waste products we get sick. We are poisoned by toxins that our own bodies have produced. What once sustained us now turns on us and causes us harm.

childhood experiences might be a source for toilet dreams

OUT WITH IT

✱ Both urine and feces can have various meanings. *Urine is seen as a form of water and symbolizes emotional "waste." It can show that a person wishes to cleanse themselves of emotional impurities.* In the sample dream the dreamer doesn't say what he needs to excrete, but when we process emotions healthily, we need time and space to do this, often in private. So it is reasonable to infer that the dreamer needs private space to "let go" of his emotions. He obviously doesn't feel that he has that space in his life at the moment.

SHAME AND GUILT

✱ Feces have a more general interpretation. Dreaming of foul matter is an indication of FEELINGS OF SHAME. There is usually some area of the dreamer's life that he doesn't feel good about, and this represents itself in dreams as foul liquids or rotten matter.
✱ This is supported in the idea that a dream of feces often relates to the lower self, and can show the person's moral or PSYCHOLOGICAL CLEANLINESS. In Freudian terms this is the Id. It is the baser nature of ourselves, the bit of us that wants instant gratification. Toilet training is one of the first socially acceptable things that we learn to do. In Freudian terms this dream shows REGRESSION, going back to

urinating in public might suggest
exhibitionist tendencies

Gross detail

For further information about the meaning of the dream, if one can bear to ask the questions, the dreamer can be asked about the size, shape, and consistency of the waste. It could show the nature of what needs eliminating. If the dreamer is flushing the toilet, this may show that they are releasing old ideas, grudges, emotions.

a time when we took pleasure from either holding or releasing feces. *Dreamers should be asked if there is anything happening in their lives that reminds them of when they were 1 or 2 years old, at the time when they were being trained in the basic rules of socially acceptable behavior.*

SHOWING OFF

What if the person is using the toilet and people are watching? In Freudian terms this shows that the dreamer is an <u>EXHIBITIONIST</u>, not caring what others think. An alternative interpretation is that the person is showing off, doing something he or she isn't supposed to.

group discussion
might suggest other
meanings

171

THEME 20: BEING LOST

✱ "I am in a strange place that I have never been to before. I am trying to find my way across it. I can't seem to get my bearings. I realize I am hopelessly lost. I feel scared and wish there were someone who could help me find my way."

being lost represents some kind of insecurity

LOCATION

The exact setting of this dream has intentionally been omitted. This is because the setting can be very important when determining what "being lost" in a dream might mean (see Theme 16).

do you need a guide?

WHERE AM I?

✱ *What does it mean to feel "lost?"* In psychological terms, being lost shows a loss of direction, motivation, or loss of purpose in life. The feeling may correspond to a situation in waking life, where the dreamer might feel that something is missing. *Depending upon the rest of the dream this could also mean losing track of some aspect of the self. These dreams can indicate that the person feels uncertain, or insecure.*

✱ Feeling lost can represent what counselors and psychologists refer to as a "CORE STATE OF BEING." In waking life people have a number of defense strategies and behaviors that hide the way they feel at the deepest level. Dreams are one of the quickest ways to discover what people really feel like when they strip off the social "PERSONA." The feeling of being lost is a regular dream theme. It could be a literal description of how they feel at a very deep level. It may represent that they are wandering aimlessly through life, with no goal or sense of belonging. *This may not be experienced on a conscious level, but is made manifest through dream content.*

✱ This leads to a Jungian perspective on "lost dreams." Many Jungian analysts believe that lost dreams show the dreamer's search for INDIVIDUATION. This is hidden in the myth about the search for the HOLY GRAIL—the grail being the whole self. So for some people this type of dream will have a deep spiritual meaning.

perhaps you can learn from being lost

TURNING LOSS INTO GAIN

Jeremy Taylor's hypothesis that all dreams come in the service of health and healing is very useful in this instance. If a person dreams of being lost, he should try to link it to his waking life and ask where he feels he has lost his way. This can be achieved by asking probing questions, which first amplify the dreams and then find out where the same feelings are in waking life. Finally, it is suggested that the dreamer ask how he could solve this problem, thus directly using dreams to improve the quality of his life.

lost dreams may be about our search for self

LOST OBJECTS

LOSS OF FAITH

Sometimes people who are struggling with their spiritual or religious beliefs may dream of being lost. For many therapists this is one of the most fundamental aspects of being a whole person, confirming how important such dreams can be.

✱ So far, general feelings of being lost have been explained, but what if it is a specific object that is lost in the dream? It is common for people to dream that they have lost their wallet, purse, or some other valuable, for example, their jewelry.

objects that we value say a lot about us, so their loss in dreams is significant

✱ *Freud's interpretation of dreams about losing valuables was that this showed in a woman the loss of her womb, femininity, or virginity (the jewels, or purse). A man losing his wallet represented a loss of virility. Other analysts would interpret the loss as representing loss of an opportunity, or some other valuable asset. This could be a job, a person, or even health.*

✱ Jungian writers, in keeping with their theories about individuation, would say that these dreams are about a loss of identity, because people keep personal things like identification papers, driver's license, and credit cards in their wallets.

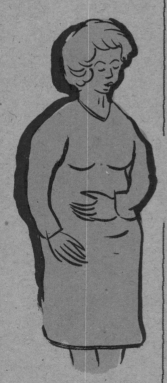

a woman's dream of losing something might be about a loss of fertility

a man losing his money can mean a loss of virility

LIFE CHANGES

✱ Research shows that dreaming of being lost occurs at times of life change. A study in 1961 investigating dreams in elderly people who had recently gone into nursing homes found that many of them dreamed of loss. *The dreams were continuations of their waking life, where they had lost homes, loved ones, and in some cases were even losing their ability to function psychologically.*

✱ We often don't acknowledge the difficulties that some people may have adapting to a major loss. When dreams of feeling lost are shared they provide the listener with a way of paying attention to the needs of others, as well as alerting the dreamer to issues in his own life.

be careful not to lose control

life changes such as moving out of your own home can bring dreams of loss

GETTING ALL THE DETAILS

Make sure that the dreamer tells you as much as she can remember about the dream. An object or familiar image may show where the feeling of loss is occurring. If this fails try Freud's "free association" technique. The dreamer should relax and say the first things that come to mind in terms of dream imagery. This method shows how the meaning of some dreams really is developed from past experiences and memories.

175

THEME 21: DREAMS OF SEX: SYMBOLIC OR EXPLICIT?

✶ Before Freud, dreams about sex were assumed to be physiologically driven rather than psychologically driven events. Indeed, scientific measures show that during REM sleep both men's and women's bodies show signs of sexual arousal.

what does it mean when you dream about sex?

it's official! sex is in your head!

sex dreams are assumed to have a psychological basis

SEX IN THE HEAD

✶ In the wake of Freud's theories, the idea that sex dreams have a psychological basis has become commonly accepted. *However, it should be appreciated that Freud believed that the sexual meaning was hidden or disguised in other dream objects, activities, or symbols.*

THE FREUDIAN SYMBOL

✶ Calvin Hall extensively recorded the various symbols that Freud believed referred to sexual activity in dreams. *Hall found 102 symbols for the penis, including horses, guns, knives, and pens.*

And 95 symbols were found for the vagina, including purses, and circular objects or containers. Hall found 55 symbols for coitus, including plowing a field, riding a horse, or going into narrow spaces.

I make it 102

there are over 100 Freudian symbols for sex

★ So sexual activity is rarely expressed directly, but hidden in the LATENT DREAM. Freud stated that if dreams directly showed sexual activity then the psychic apparatus that transforms the content of the dream into its latent form had not worked effectively. Freud used the defense mechanism of CONDENSATION to show how seemingly irrelevant objects could hold many levels of meaning. *This is how the damaging material was hidden from the conscious mind. In other words, having explicitly sexual dreams meant the mind wasn't doing its job properly. We should never recall sex dreams because they may cause psychological harm.*

you must not recall your sex dreams!

according to Freud, remembering a sex dream is bad for your psychological health

Having sex with an unexpected lover

Freud would argue that this was a repressed wish to have sex with someone that the dreamer knows but with whom sex is forbidden. On the other hand, Carl Jung would argue that such a dream shows a need for balance with an unexpected aspect of the anima/animus archetype. A Gestalt proposition would be that the lover is a sealed-off part of the dreamer, indicating a need for unity with this part of the self.

177

A CHALLENGE TO FREUD

✱ A serious contradiction to Freud's theory is contained in the following question: *Why, if sex is so harmful to the mind that it is normally disguised, do we dream about it directly?*

kings and queens in sex dreams
represent your parents

✱ The obvious answer is because Freud got it wrong! One of the most widely taken-for-granted assumptions in dream interpretation is that the symbols contained in dreams stand for something else, so there can be little argument with this aspect of what Freud had to say. *However, it is possible and probable that sometimes the meaning of a dream is literal—we dream about sex because we are attracted to the person we are dreaming about, or because we don't*

SEX WITH FAMOUS PEOPLE

Having sex with a king or a queen might be representative of sex with one's parents—a Freudian interpretation. Jungian analysts comment that sex with famous people shows the state of the dreamer's ego. It could show that the dreamer is uniting with an overinflated part of himself. The nature of the celebrity could shed more light on which part of the self applies. If you find yourself engaged in a sexual act with a famous person it is important to ask what the sex is actually like! If the dreamer reports feeling dominated, Ann Faraday suggests that it might be appropriate to initiate a "top dog versus underdog" dialogue (see page 83).

what does your dream
say about you?

have an active sex life and dreaming compensates for this.

✱ In these terms the nature and function of dreams is <u>MULTIDIMENSIONAL</u>. This is one of the things that makes them so interesting. Using this approach we can treat sex the way we treat any other dream symbol, and ask what the act of sex represents other than its literal meaning.

✱ Studies using large number of dreams have shown that men tend to dream of having spontaneous sex with stereotypically "beautiful" women whom they don't know, while women dream more of romantic encounters with people they know or with whom they are involved .

sex, it's great

dreams about
sex may have a
positive effect
on your sex life

Having sex with a coworker or friend

Have you ever had a dream in which you were surprised to find yourself having sex with a friend or coworker? This type of sex dream can come as real shock, especially if the dreamer isn't consciously aware of being attracted to the other person. What quality is it that the dreamer wants to unite with, or is this a case of literal attraction?

dreaming about
someone at
work might
suggest a
secret
attraction

179

some sex dreams can
be very distressing

Sex with a member of the same sex

Delaney says that these dreams do not necessarily mean that the dreamer is gay. The lover can represent qualities that the dreamer aspires to. Freud would claim that this does show homosexual tendencies. But Jung would say that the dreamer needs to assimilate more of his or her same-sex qualities into their daily living, that the dream may show a need for balance. Dreams of having a sexual encounter with the same sex can be disturbing for heterosexuals. Similarly, it has been reported that gays and lesbians feel equally disturbed when they dream of having sex with a member of the opposite sex.

THEME 22: DREAMS OF SEX: THE DOWNSIDE

✶ Both men and women can have dreams where they feel coerced or forced into sex with a dream character. For some dreamers this is a waking sexual fantasy, played out during dreams. However, this type of dream can also be very distressing. The dreamer often wakes with a racing heart, and the feeling that something terrible is about to happen.

DOMINATION

✶ For some unfortunate people it already has—a form of traumatic nightmare, where such dreams are a replay of an event that has taken place. For others, though, there is no literal explanation, there is no wish for forceful sex or domination. *What possible explanations are there for such dreams?*

a dream may reflect some previous trauma

that's so shocking

dreams can offer
a glimpse into
your mind

Sex with a past lover

This can indicate unfinished business in a relationship. It can in some instances be a pleasant way to remember an old lover. This appears to be especially true for women, who dream of past lovers more frequently than men.

sex dreams are not always positive

★ Gayle Delaney believes that these dreams symbolize "UNITY." In this case it may be that the dreamer wishes to deepen an existing connection, or assimilate into himself some aspect of a character that he admires. *If it is someone that the dreamer works with, is there the possibility of uniting for some project, that could further the development of both parties?*
★ *Ann Faraday, on the other hand, believes that this can be a straight-forward outward-looking type of dream —a warning, not to be too blunt, that they may be about to be "shafted" in some way. This highlights the point that sexual dreams might not always have a positive meaning.*

PICK 'N' MIX

Dreams don't tell us our sexual orientation but Bogart says that "To be sexually mature means to be wise about the full range sexuality and sexual choices." Dreams do seem to provide a range of possibilities!

Other aspects of sex dreams

The language used to describe the act may be significant. There are many uses of "sex" in our language, so a sexual reference may have other meanings. For example, sex dreams may be metaphors for being:
Excited—*does this apply to an area of life?*
Worked up—*could be any area of emotional arousal.*
Turned on—*not just physically but mentally.*
Intimately involved—*in a project or a relationship.*
Frustrated—*could relate to any area of life, not just the romantic or sexual arena.*
Impotent—*loss of power*

It may help to look at who the lover is. Does he have some qualities that the dreamer wants, or dislikes? What is the sex like? Is this degree of passion missing in her life? Another possibility is that the dream actually represents the dreamer's attitude toward sex.

DREAMS AND SEXUAL ABUSE

* *It is important to remember that the relationship between dreams and waking life is a two-way interaction. As waking life affects dreams, so dreams can affect waking life.*

dreams about sex with a family member are very disturbing

* It may be that the first hint that someone has that they have been abused will be in the form of a dream. They may dream about having sexual contact with a member of the family or another trusted person. This may frighten the person so much they feel sure that it has happened.

A WARNING

* *A dream should never be the basis for telling someone that they have been abused. Anyone—a doctor, a therapist, or a friend—who does this is not acting responsibly.* Dreams *can* indicate that abuse has occurred, but it will rarely be in the literal form described above.

✱ If a person suspects he or she has been abused he should seek help from an appropriate source, and the abuse should be verified through means other than dream content. *There is a growing body of evidence that false memories can be constructed when dream content is misperceived as reality.*

✱ *Some research studies have investigated the dreams of women survivors of sexual abuse. Abuse dreams contain references to death of the self, and to the self or other dream characters being chased or attacked. The dreamer often*

dreams are not a reliable source of evidence

CAUSE FOR CONCERN

When sex is involved in abuse dreams it often starts off as pleasant and ends up being violent. The general feeling is one of helplessness and loss of control. A cause for concern would be if these dream were recurring, or the only type of dream or nightmare that was recalled.

you need help

people should seek help from an appropriate source if abuse is suspected

reports being choked, trapped, or paralyzed, or experiencing some other type of physical harm. There is frequently a lot of bloodshed. Often snakes or worms are present in the dream environment. This type of dream is sometimes called a "marker dream."

snakes are often a feature of abuse dreams

THEME 23: EMOTIONS IN DREAMS

* For many people, the emotional tone of a dream is its most prominent element. Try to recall the first dream you can ever remember having. Next, try to recall the most emotionally powerful dream that you ever had. Finally, try to remember the most frightening dream you have ever had. For about three quarters of people, the dreams that they recall will be unpleasant, and for a large number they may all be the same dream.

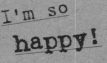

I'm so **happy!**

LETTING YOUR FEELINGS OUT

* It has been largely accepted that the most probable function of dreams is to process emotional information. *This appears to be especially true at times of great emotional or psychological distress.*

* It is possible to describe the emotional content of dreams by collecting and analyzing the content of the dream reports. *Hall and Van de Castle have said that only one in three dreams contain emotion. However, Merritt, Stickgold, Pace-Schott, and Hobson changed the way they asked the dreamer questions, and showed that the number*

your emotions in dreams are as important as the events that occur

of emotions reported in dreams increased tenfold from Hall and Van de Castle's original study. Despite their methodological differences, both studies agree that the most common emotion experienced during dreaming is fear.

✱ In 1996, a ground-breaking study was conducted looking at activity in the brain during sleep. A French neurologist took pictures of men's brains and mapped the activity in those who reported dreaming when they woke up. *He found that during REM sleep, the sleep stage most associated with dreaming, the amygdaloid complex and other areas of the brain associated with processing emotional memories were the most active. This tends to suggest what many psychologists have intuitively known for years: that dreaming serves an emotional function.*

brain scans have revealed what is happening when we dream

MEN'S AND WOMEN'S EMOTIONAL EXPERIENCE DURING DREAMS

	Men	Women
Fear	35%	40%
Anger	12%	9%
Confusion	23%	20%
Sadness	19%	13%
Happiness	21%	18%

I must NOT get emotional before bed

women report emotional dreams more than men

185

THE EMOTIONAL EFFECT OF DREAMS

it's affected my whole life

★ *Have you ever had a dream that was emotionally so intense or profound that it has had an impact on your waking life?* Don Kuiken, a Canadian researcher, spent considerable time studying such dreams, and he found that a lot of people had emotionally intense dreams that affected their waking lives, sometimes for days afterward. *He identified five categories of dreams, four of which are marked by their emotional content.*

1. Existential dreams—These dreams were emotionally distressing, and related to separation and loss. They felt very real and contained many references to the body and other types of SENSORY AWARENESS (vision, touch, sound). The dreamer often mentioned feeling self-awareness in the dream. The dreams ended with intense emotion that continued into the next waking period.

2. Anxiety dreams—These dreams contained intense fear. The dreamer usually tried to avoid harm, but often found he or she couldn't move. There was little self-awareness in these dreams. The person was often awakened by terror.

USING DREAMS

Kuiken asked which dreams had the most impact in terms of self-development. People said that existential dreams were the most significant in this respect, suggesting that unpleasant emotional dreams really do have the most impact on our lives. This suggests that we should embrace such dreams and use them to help us improve our lives.

exam dreams are a type of anxiety dream

3. Transcendent dreams—Characterized by strong, joyful emotions. The dreamer often reported being able to perform SUPERHUMAN or even MAGICAL acts, performed with vigor and energy, leaving the dreamer feeling energized.

some dreams have no significant emotional content or images

4. Alienation dreams—Contained reports of feeling sad and downhearted, but also (sometimes) shifts in emotional experience through the dream. *The main theme was often rejection. These dreams contained clear memories of movement but few other sensory events.*

5. Mundane dreams—Those dreams that didn't contain strong emotion or activity, or appear to have any benefit for the dreamer.

Dream types

Don Kuiken believes that there are naturally occurring dream types. This is potentially very important because it may mean that all the themes outlined here have some kind of evolutionary importance. Here are some examples of themes matched with their dream types:

1. Existential dreams—dying or nearly dying, losing a wallet or purse, giving birth

2. Anxiety dreams—taking an exam, missing a train, being chased, falling

3. Transcendent dreams—flying dreams, overcoming adversity, some sexual dreams

4. Alienation dreams—being lost in dream landscapes

5. Mundane dreams—these would be dreams that we recall but that don't have much emotional impact.

DO DREAMS HAVE MEANING?

* The interpretations presented here suggest that dreams *do* have meaning. The next question, though, is whether that meaning is intended in the dreaming process or whether it is inferred from a series of possibly random images after the dreamer awakens. Freud and Jung, and to a lesser extent Delaney and Faraday, all argue that dream content is determined by the waking life of the dreamer. Hall argues that dreams literally reflect the dreamer's view of the world.

dreams reflect
the dreamer's
view of the
world

THE MAIN ISSUE?

* Perhaps the most sensible proposition of all is made by William Domhoff. He states that the meaning of dreams is not the main issue. *What is relevant is the meaning we place upon dreams after we wake up. Because we think they have meaning—they do!* Nearly all the symbols, metaphors, and sayings used in the

What dreams do

Dreams do seem to perform some type of emotional-processing function. They provide an arena where we can act out our worst unconscious fears, while staying safe, embraced in the arms of sleep. It also appears that emotionally unpleasant dreams, containing existential life themes, also contain the greatest possibility for changing one's waking life.
It has also been clearly shown that waking life affects dreams. This is apparent in the analysis of clinical situations where dreams are considered— for example, in special circumstances like trauma, abuse, or sleep anomalies such as sleep paralysis.

interpretations are only understood when they are analyzed in terms of what they mean to the individual as waking symbols.

it's a lot to think about

CONCLUSIONS

★ Dream symbols can be understood. The researchers mentioned here, both past and present, have offered various, and sometimes very different, interpretations of what universal and common dream themes mean. *What is obvious is that dream content reflects information about the psychological, emotional, physical, and spiritual state of the dreamer—and also about any important external events that are taking place in the dreamer's life. This can include relationship breakups, work issues, or the life-stage development of the dreamer.*

★ So dreaming and waking are inextricably linked, a transactional process that takes us from one period of wakefulness into another, and from one period of sleep back into the waking state. Thus a SYNERGY is formed where one state of consciousness is not as rich without the other.

dreaming is a means of processing emotions

it is possible to interpret dreams

Learning from your dreams

Reading about these different methods of analyzing dreams, you may prefer one or another, in theory or in practice, or you may like the idea of trying several different methods. Whatever your preference, every dream, pleasant or terrifying, should be used to illuminate life and further self-development.

*A

advice dreams 130
aggressive dreams 23, 144-7
alienation dreams 187
alpha rhythm 10, 11
amplification 80, 81
angels 155
Anima/Animus 78-9, 105
animals 14-17, 19, 116-19, 144-5
anxiety 22, 24-7, 90, 145, 186-7
archetypes 78-9, 95, 139, 152-3
Aristotle 32, 34-5
Aserinsky, Eugene 10
Assyrians 28, 29
astral projection 125
attack dreams 144-7
autonomic nervous system 8, 9

*B

big dreams 79, 139
birth, dreams of 136-9
boats 140
brain 10-11, 15-23, 44-7

*C

cars 140, 160-1
castration complex 109, 117
chase dreams 145, 148-51
children's dreams 22-7, 34-5, 119
China 37
circadian rhythms 6, 7
clothing in dreams 102, 103
collective unconscious 43, 77
communication problems 162
compensation theory 146-7
computers
  dream models 44-5
  imagery 162
condensation 177
consciousness 8-9, 36-7, 42, 52-3,
  76-7, 110
content analysis 92-3, 94, 159
contrary wishes 101
creative dreams 56-65
Crick, Francis 18, 46-7, 69

*D

death 7, 37, 128-35, 142
Delaney, Gayle 86-7, 134
  dream settings 158
  exam dreams 99
  falling dreams 121
  famous people in dreams 115
  flying dreams 127

giving birth in dreams 137
public nakedness dreams 102
sexual dreams 180, 181
water dreams 167
delta waves 11
Dement, William 10, 13, 56
demons 152-5
devil 38-9
"dictionary" theory 71, 73
Domhoff, William 98, 188
dopamine 21
dream diagrams 86
dream interviews 86-7
dream work 74, 75
drugs 91
dustbin theory 46-7

*E

eating disorders 112-13, 114
EEG see electroencephalogram
ego 144
Egyptians 29
Electra complex 108
electroencephalogram (EEG) 10-11
emotions 40-1, 53, 93, 156-7,
  165-6, 170; 184-7
empty chair technique 82-3, 114
epiphenomenalism 68, 69
Europe 38-9
Evans, Christopher 44-5, 46
exam dreams 96-9
existentialism 84, 85, 186, 187

*F

feces 170-1
faith, loss of 174
falling, dreams of 120-3
falling asleep 13
false awakenings 55
famous people dreams 112-15, 178
Faraday, Ann 84-5, 120, 126-7,
  135, 143, 178, 181
fear 24-7, 123, 148, 185
Fenwick, Peter 49, 52, 54, 55
flying, dreams of 124-7
food 25, 34
free association 41, 74, 81, 175
Freud, Sigmund 39-43, 74-5, 77,
  81, 108
  animals in dreams 117, 118
  attack dreams 146
  broken machine dreams 163
  chase dreams 149
  death dreams 132-3

exam dreams 97-8
falling dreams 122, 123
famous people dreams 115
flying dreams 126
giving birth in dreams 138-9
loss 174
personality elements 144
public nakedness dreams 101
sex-change dreams 106
sexual dreams 176-7, 178, 180
toilet dreams 170-1
tooth loss dreams 109
transport dreams 142-3
traumatic dreams 90
water dreams 164
functions of dreams 14-19, 42, 77, 184

G
gender issues 23, 104-7, 119
Gestalt therapy 82-3, 85, 114, 147, 177
God 38-9
gods 29, 30-1, 37, 154
Greece, Ancient 7, 30-5
grief process 128-31
group therapy 88-9, 91, 146
guilt 170-1

H
Hall, Calvin 72-3, 92-3, 98, 109, 144-5, 159, 176-7, 184
Hartmann, Ernest 149, 156-7
hippocampus 15, 16, 17
Hippocrates 32-3, 34
homeostatic system 14, 15
homes 158-9
homosexual dreams 180
honoring dreams 110

I
id 144
illness 9, 30-3, 35, 125, 180-1
imagery rehearsal treatment 91
incorporation 168
incubation 30, 37
incubus 67
India 36-7
individuation 78-9, 139, 142, 173
insects 117
inspiration 62-5
interlocking procedures 45
interpretation of dreams 29, 66-93, 95-189

J
Jung, Carl 43, 71, 76-81
animals in dreams 119
attack dreams 146-7
chase dreams 149, 150
death dreams 132, 133
dream settings 159
exam dreams 99
famous people dreams 115
giving birth in dreams 139
loss 174
"lost" dreams 173
monster dreams 152-3
sex-change dreams 104-5
sexual dreams 177, 178, 180
transport dreams 142
water dreams 165

K
Kleitman, Nathaniel 10
Kubla Khan 62-3

L
latent dreams 74, 75, 177
libido 142
little dreams 79
loss 109, 110-11, 174-5
"lost" dreams 172-5
lucid dreams 48-55, 124-5, 150

M
machines
brain analogy 44-7
broken 160-3
manifest dreams 74, 75, 76, 81
meaning of dreams 70-1, 188-9
memory 16-20, 57
men 13
Anima/Animus 78-9
birth issues 136-7, 139
dream content 92-3
dream settings 159
emotions in dreams 185
flying dreams 126
public nakedness dreams 100
sexual dreams 179
mental illness 25, 40-1, 57, 75
metaphors 72, 99, 157, 188-9
Middle Ages 38-9
Mitchison, Graeme 18, 46, 69
monsters 152-5
mountains 158
mundane dreams 187

*N

nakedness, dreams of 100-3
neocortex 18, 19
neural networks 46-7
neuronal gating 17
Newman, Ted 44-5
night terrors 26-7
nightmares 24-5, 27, 149

*P

paralysis 12, 15, 66, 67, 154
paranormal dreams 29, 30-1, 66-7
Perls, Fritz 72, 82-3, 113
persona 78, 104-5
personality, Freudian model 144
phyletic memory 19
planes 141
Plato 32, 33, 34
precognitive dreams 120, 130
pregnancy 138, 139
problem solving 56-61
prodromal dreams 32-3, 125, 160
psychoanalysis 41

*R

recurring dreams 148, 149
regression 158, 164
REM sleep 10-17, 20-3, 45
    dustbin theory 47
    functions 15-17, 19, 185
    nightmares 27
    problems 56-7
REM rebound 7
"reversal" 146
Romantic era 39

*S

Saint-Denys, Hervey de 49, 150
Schatzman, Morton 57-9
Seigel, Alan 111, 138, 139
serpents 154-5
settings, dream 156-9, 172
sex-change dreams 104-7
sexual abuse 182-3
sexual dreams 67, 142-3, 176-83
sexual identity disorder 107
sexuality 40-1, 42
Shadow 78, 150, 153
sleep paralysis 66, 67, 154
snakes 118-19, 154-5
soul 7, 37
spirits 28, 37
suicide dreams 134-5
superego 144, 145

survival behavior 16
swimming dreams 164-7
symbolism 77, 80, 122, 138-9,
    176-9, 188-9

*T

Taylor, Jeremy 73, 133, 134, 173
telephone imagery 131, 162-3
Thanatos 31, 142
themes 29, 94-189
theta rhythm 11, 15, 16, 17
"toilet" dreams 168-71
tooth loss, dreams of 108-11
"top dog" 83
topographical theories 77
trains 140-2, 143
transcendent dreams 187
transport dreams 140-3
traumatic dreams 90

*U

Ullman, Montague 88-9, 91
unconscious mind 8-9, 39, 42-3,
    74-8, 165
underdog 83
unity 181
universal dreams 29, 94-5, 122-3
unlearning 47
urine 170

*V

Van de Castle, Robert 92-3, 103,
    121, 145, 159, 184

*W

waking up 27, 55
water dreams 164-7
Winson, Jonathon 16-20
wish fulfilment 42, 74-5, 97, 114,
    132-3, 142-3
women
    Anima/Animus 78-9
    birth issues 136-7, 138
    broken machine dreams 162-3
    dream content 92-3
    dream settings 159
    emotions in dreams 185
    falling dreams 122
    flying dreams 126
    sexual dreams 179
    sexuality 41

*Y

yoga 36, 53